Emotional Overeating

How to Master and Stop Emotional Eating and Compulsive Overeating.

Elisabeth Walker

© **Copyright 2022 by Elisabeth Walker - All rights reserved.**

This document is geared towards providing exact and reliable information in regard to the topic and issue covered.

- From a Declaration of Principles which was accepted and approved equally by a Committee of the American Bar Association and a Committee of Publishers and Associations.
In no way is it legal to reproduce, duplicate, or transmit any part of this document in either electronic means or in printed format. All rights reserved.
The information provided herein is stated to be truthful and consistent, in that any liability, in terms of inattention or otherwise, by any usage or abuse of any policies, processes, or directions contained within is the solitary and utter responsibility of the recipient reader. Under no circumstances will any legal responsibility or blame be held against the publisher for any reparation, damages, or monetary loss due to the information herein, either directly or indirectly.
Respective authors own all copyrights not held by the publisher.
The information herein is offered for informational purposes solely and is universal as so. The presentation of the information is without contract or any type of guarantee assurance.
The trademarks that are used are without any consent, and the publication of the trademark is without permission or backing by the trademark owner. All trademarks and brands within this book are for clarifying purposes only and are owned by the owners themselves, not affiliated with this document.

Table of Contents

Introduction 5

Chapter 1. You Need Help: Ending Your Emotional Eating Without Going on another Diet 8

Chapter 2. Accepting the Idea of Acceptance 13

Chapter 3. Stress and Eating Addiction 25

Chapter 4. Superficial Behaviors – What Should You Do To Stop Them 33

Chapter 5. Food as Your Solace to Emotional Needs 41

Chapter 6. Hunger, Belly, Brain 49

Chapter 7. Eating Disorders 62

Chapter 8. The Friend You Need The Most Now is YOU 66

Chapter 9. Finding Your True Self 74

Chapter 10. Your Road to Recovery 80

Chapter 11. Inner Nurturing Forever 92

Conclusion 102

Introduction

Do you wake up each morning dreading how the day will turn out to be and what will trigger the 'emotional eating' switch again?

Are you unable to achieve your weight loss goals no matter how many times you change your diet?

Do you feel guilty after every meal? Do you feel miserable after eating? If yes, then there is something wrong here. Eating is supposed to be a pleasurable experience and you should actually feel good after a nice meal. Even if you are not feeling 'on top of the world' after your meal, you should certainly not feel guilty but if you are feeling guilty after eating, then obviously something is wrong!

- Emotional eating is one of the primary causes of obesity.

- Emotional eating is prevalent in all age groups – children, teen, adults and the elderly.

- As opposed to what most of us believe, emotional eating is not just limited to negative emotions. Even positive emotions can set you on an eating binge.

- Emotional eating does not only put you out of shape making it almost impossible for you to enjoy your beach vacations in your bikini, but it also puts you through serious health risks.

Yes, all these are true, but the good news is that you could break free from your emotional eating habits. Yes, you can have control and stop emotional eating and compulsive eating habits.

One of the reasons why most of us struggle to overcome our binge eating disorder is that we are made to believe that overcoming this issue is not easy. Unfortunately, we tend to believe this and thereby make it difficult for ourselves. While this is the case with some of us, a good number of us live in denial. We are not ready to accept that we are binging. We just like to believe that it is just an occasional indulgence. As long as you are planning to wear these facades, nothing will change.

How many times have you changed your diet programs and your workout regimes without success?

Do you want to continue experiencing the same issues that you are experiencing with your binging even though you are not ready to accept the fact that you are an emotional overeater, or do you want to address the issues at hand by taking an honest approach?

In the following pages, we will be exploring how we are wired to respond in a certain way, the reason why we behave the way we behave. We will find out whether we have a choice to express our emotions differently or are we doomed with pre-set responses to our emotions. You will also understand the power of acceptance and how it could set you on the path to recovery.

You just need to learn how to rewire a few things and start looking for the solutions in the right places. If the cause of obesity is of psychological nature, then dietary changes are not going to really help you achieve your weight loss goals. You need to search where you lost it... You need to rather look for your weight loss solutions by putting together the missing pieces.

Your recovery or success will not depend merely with the knowledge and insights that you are likely to gain by reading this book but only by committing to the changes recommended in the following pages.

Vow to yourself that you will master and stop emotional eating and compulsive eating because you know that it is now within your control and that you will be able to achieve your goals without a grain of doubt as long as you are willing to put your heart and mind into it.

Chapter 1
You Need Help: Ending Your Emotional Eating Without Going on another Diet

Hunger, the most basic drives of all human drives, is meant to sustain human life on this planet. Without the hunger drive, we would not have survived all these years as a species. Hunger and eating are pure existential matters, we know it! You wish that it stopped at that but unfortunately, it does not. Human existence is a lot more complex than the rest of the animal existence.

It is natural or normal if your eating response is triggered by the biological switch. With emotional eating, what happens is your urge to eat is not triggered by the biological switch it is rather turned on by psychological triggers. This is where the challenges begin.

If you are experiencing excess hunger because of some hormonal imbalance or other physical reasons, you can pop in a few pills to suppress your hunger or get some other medical treatment to deal with the issue. If you experience abnormal hunger pangs because of biological reasons, you could choose diet plans that will make you feel full with smaller portions of food, but all those efforts will not work with emotional eating because the issue does not fit in the physical or biological framework.

Paying thousands of dollars to a personal trainer for providing you with a customized workout plan will not work either and neither will be subscribing to any other type of weight loss program. Listing all those things that won't work is definitely not to make you feel how bleak the situation is, but it is to help you understand that 'YOU NEED HELP'.

You might say, 'but I have been trying to get help from almost everyone I meet, try to get weight loss tips, dietary food tips and workout tips'. You may even follow all these tips conscientiously, but with no results. If you have been failing to overcome your obesity issues all along, then the chances are high that you are looking for your help in the wrong places. Unless and until you hit the right switch, you cannot turn things around. You want to change things for sure and that is why this e-book is in your hands.

Your switch is in understanding your triggers and in asking the right questions. What is making you go on an eating binge?

When exactly does it start?

What exactly happens just before you reach for food when you are not really hungry?

How frequently does it happen?

If you are an emotional eater, then the answers to the above questions will clearly point to emotional or psychological factors. If it does, then instead of denying and trying to explain away your behavior, just surrender to it.

"Acceptance could be your road to recovery."

Understanding Emotions and Eating Habits

Let us first list the series of emotions/situations that are found to most commonly trigger binging in people who suffer an emotional eating disorder.

Feeling / experiencing one or more of these could trigger binging:

- Depressed
- Sad
- Angry
- Let down
- Lonely
- Confused
- Bored
- Afraid
- Failure
- Grief
- Loss of purpose in life
- Extremely happy

With any of the above emotions or situations, do you do one or more of the following? We are not talking of occasional behaviors, rather frequent episodes of such behaviors and repeating patterns.

- Go to a huge food shopping
- Eating huge meals within short intervals without physical hunger
- Serve yourself abnormally large portions of food
- Eat extremely fast
- Hiding or sneaking food in unusual places

Feel you are losing control and not able to stop eating even when you feel full and want to stop

If you could identify with the above responses to the emotions that we have listed above, then it is very likely that you are an emotional eater and it is crucial that you accept it without denying it and thereby speed up your own recovery.

Only when you review your own eating patterns, you will be able to understand what is happening to you. Without this self-analysis, you will not be in a position to identify the negative eating patterns in your life and without identifying such patterns, you will not be able to get to the end of the tunnel. Once you understand that there are negative eating patterns triggered by emotional causes, then it is time to be honest with yourself and accept it. If you are going to deny that you are not an emotional eater, it is not going to do you any good and you would only be going to be making several 'failing attempts' to lose weight through dieting and through countless weight loss programs. The longer you deny the farther you would move from the solution.

"Honesty is your key to success in achieving your weight loss goals."

Unless you address the core issues, your eating patterns will not change and if you want to change the eating patterns, you need to reset the switches. If you have been failing all along, it is not because you did not care or because you were not desperate enough for things to change. Despite all your frantic efforts, you have not been able to achieve your goals and it is a clear sign that all your efforts were misguided. It need not be the case any longer. You can decide to change things for good now and take some decisive measures towards achieving your goals. If it were to be an impossible feat, no one would have managed to turn things around in their life and reclaim a normal lifestyle. Thousands of people have already managed to overcome binging and you too will be able to come out colorfully. Everything starts with acceptance and that is the journey you will embrace. No more binging and no more failed attempts.

Chapter 2
Accepting the Idea of Acceptance

You need some kind of intervention to overcome your obesity issues; it is not possible to get back to shape without such well-tailored interventions. The primary question is where should this intervention start? The starting point, of course, is 'you' and 'your acceptance.' Unless and until you reach the state of acceptance, have the honesty and courage to call 'a spade a spade,' you are not going to make any progress in terms of achieving healthy eating habits and leading a healthy life.

Once you understand and accept how the idea of acceptance works, make a conscious decision to embrace this idea, you will be able to experience a dramatic shift within. This inner shift is one of the most essential ingredients for your success.

Acceptance can work miracles and it will help you get to the state of "mindfulness" which you have been resisting all along. When you are binging you unconsciously flooded your mind with as many distractions as possible, overloading your senses so that you do not have to face the fact that is staring at you squarely. Distraction was probably your defense mechanism to avert the sense of guilt when you were binging.

It is very interesting to see the interplay of emotions and the emotional intelligence in the emotional eating or binging episodes. If the sense of guilt is strong enough, it will create a powerful switch for you to stop binging. Emotional intelligence, when not distracted with sensory overload, would aid in monitoring the effects of your emotions, which in turn would induce the state of mindfulness and self-awareness. As it happens with most people while binging, you were probably busy watching your favorite TV show or playing your favorite game on the internet. As a result, all possibilities of mindfulness and self-awareness are thwarted.

If you are wondering why you have not made any attempt to move into the state of mindfulness and self-awareness, then the answer is simple, you have not shifted to the state of acceptance in the first place. I would restate this countless times; everything starts with acceptance of your own state instead of living in denial. You have overeating issues and you need help!

Now that you are made aware of the dynamics involved, you are in a much better position than where you were when we started. All that you need to do now is to reverse engineer things. Most of your problems would be taken care once you let your emotional intelligence to monitor your emotions and it will help your brain to build a strong defense against the unhealthy and inappropriate response.

In order to reverse engineer the whole process, you may need a few tools and one of the most important tools is 'Mindfulness'. Invest your time and energy on learning how to induce a 'mindful' state at will. We are trained, rather conditioned to think that single-minded focus and attention to things is unproductive. We invented the term multi-tasking as an effort to euphemistically make chronic-distraction more acceptable and to feel comfortable with that state.

Multi-tasking is not a bad word! Unfortunately, we prefer to consider the distracted state as multi-tasking and end up in an unending chatter, which clouds our mind and hampers our ability to monitor the emotions. What you need now first and foremost once you are in the state of acceptance are some powerful tools, techniques and strategies to induce the state of mindfulness. This state of mindfulness will help you keep a close tab on your emotions and your responses to those emotions so that you may take the necessary corrective measures to regulate those responses.

Pay attention to the flow of thoughts when you are binging. If you shut down all the noises both internal and external, which you create for yourself, you will be in a better position to pay attention to your feelings when you are about to traverse into the state of binging.

In this journey to recovery, you need to expect four stages and that is how normally a successful shift is made to the desired state.

Stage 1: Initially, you were in a state of denial. You did not know what was happening to you and why you were behaving in the way you were behaving. You were not even aware that your overeating response was triggered and controlled by your emotions and that was why you have been taking all the wrong efforts like, continually changing your diets hoping to reduce weight. This is when you were least successful in achieving your goal and in sustaining your own efforts to change your eating habits.

Stage 2: You are now in a state of acceptance and mindfulness. This is when you learn to monitor your own feelings and your inner states while binging. The emotional trigger is still powerful at this stage. You still do not know you are sliding into binging. However, once the response sets in, you catch yourself in the act of binging. Followed by this awareness you regulate your response and hopefully reduce the food intake once the awareness kicks in.

Stage 3: The emotional triggers are still powerful but in this third stage. What happens here is that you catch yourself at the nick of the moment just before you get into that 'negative response state' and thereby avoid binging. It is important to note here that the trigger is still active, but the only difference is that your awareness level is heightened enough to stop before the usual negative response.

Stage 4: This is the state of victory. The trigger loses its power and it can no more be considered a trigger. You do not run away from those emotions, which have been triggering your binging. You will continue to be stressed whenever you are stretched beyond limits. You will feel sad whenever such a response is appropriate. You will experience loneliness from time to time. All these emotional states will no more force you to reach out for food as a measure to overcome the emotional state that is troubling you.

As you can easily guess, it takes time for people to move from Stage 1 to Stage 4. You cannot expect yourself to change overnight. This nonetheless does not mean that one cannot change overnight. However, what we are discussing here is about how a majority of people pan out in this journey.

When you are going through this journey of recovery, pay close attention to your emotions. This, of course, requires you to constantly be in a state of mindfulness.

What are your emotions? Identify your emotions. As social beings, we are constantly going to be exposed to various external factors, which are going to influence our emotions. We need to quickly clarify here by the word 'emotion/emotions' we do not necessarily mean 'negative emotions' the word 'emotion / emotions' is a neutral term. In your interaction with others, you could undergo a series of emotional states both good and bad. You will keep switching from one emotional state to the other and this cycle continues unendingly all through the day. There is not a single moment whereby we are completely free of emotions. Just keep track of these emotions. You do not have to do anything about them, just keep labeling them. By labeling, I do not mean calling them good or bad but just keep acknowledging your emotional state. This will help you gain control or regulate those emotions. Your goal is not to remain emotionless because an emotionless existence will make you nothing but a vegetable. You are not going to desire for such a vegetable existence.

What do your emotions tell you? Our 'emotion' is not the real issue but how we interpret is what makes things problematic. For example, when you are experiencing grief it could either tell you how much you loved the person, or it could tell you that no one could be trusted because everyone would leave you behind someday. Each one of us is free to interpret our emotions and give meaning to them in the way we like based on what we have been trained into and based on our past experience. Instead of trying to explore, which is the most appropriate interpretation or the correct interpretation, ask yourself a little different question. Is your interpretation or way of looking at things really useful for you at this point in time in your life? Give yourself an honest response and you will be in a better position to make the required changes.

How do you learn to express your emotions? All of us are put through different schools when it comes to learning to express our emotions. Whether you accept it or not, whether you like it or not, we learn to express our emotions and each one of us has learned to do it differently and that is why there are as many ways of expressing the emotions as there are people. It would prove to be insightful to learn and understand how we learn to express our emotions.

We learn to express our emotions from our parents, guardians, teachers, siblings and whoever has been in a position to exert control over us when we were young. No one lives in a perfect world to have everyone around them expressing their emotions in the perfect way in which they should. As a result, most of us invariably grow up with a wrong framework when it comes to expressing our emotions. Some of them get instilled deeply making it challenging to change. There are some other expressions of emotions that we learned from the world around us got changed, got tweaked and perfected itself based on our further learnings on what worked for us. The key term to note here is 'what worked for us'. Yes, if it were not to work for us, we would have changed those expressions a long time ago. Every time it worked, we got it reinforced and believed that is the best way to express one's emotions. However, when life situations change those expressions are no more useful, but they are so hard-wired in us we are unable to change them even when we know that they are no more useful. Emotional eating could be one such behavior among those learned behaviors.

A little while ago, I invited you to ask yourself an important question about your interpretation of the emotions you are experiencing: "Is it useful?"

I invite you to ask the same question again with expressions of your emotions: "Is it useful?"

You should continue doing something only when it is, if it is useful. It would be imprudent holding on the behaviors that are no more useful.

One of the most important insights that is going to help you here is that, if all your expressions of emotions are learned expressions, don't you think that you can also unlearn them? In other words, you have a choice. Your responses or expressions do not have to be the way they are now. There is more than one way to express your emotions and if your current way of expressing your emotions is not going to be useful, more so if it is going to harm you, then use the choices you have at hand or at least acknowledge that you have choices before you and explore those options instead of continuing as if you are doomed without any option.

Emotional Regulation

All along, you never paid attention to how you are expressing your emotions. From now on, you will closely monitor your expressions for various emotions. This is certainly going to be a very good start for you. If you can monitor your responses or your expressions, you can also regulate them.

Why is emotional regulation important?

Without gaining control over your emotions, it is not possible to change your eating response associated with it. Just imagine for a moment whereby a world in which no one controls their emotions... it is scary right? It would be chaotic. On the one side, there would be fanfares of achievement and success and on the other side wailing and lamenting without cessation. Now also all these things co-exist but in a highly regulated way. If these emotions were let out of control, then normal life would certainly not be possible, life on this planet would be a lot different and absolutely unbearable. When you go on binging that is what happens momentarily. You lose control of the expression of your emotions and get yourself sucked into this wrongly learned, a negative response that is not only not useful but also highly damaging and harmful to you. Emotional regulation is undoubtedly important if you want to change things for the better. Rather than emotional regulation, your expressions of those emotions are what need to be regulated. When something extremely good happens in your life, how do you feel 'less happy'? You cannot control the intensity of your happiness, but you can certainly regulate or control your response and your expression of such an emotional state. The same applies to all the negative emotions too.

Why Can't I Manage My Emotions?

Emotions are natural human responses. Emotions in themselves have their own specific primitive goals to achieve and they are meant to achieve two such important goals, one is to make us thrive in situations that are favorable and to protect us from unfavorable situations. In other words, we are wired to experience these emotions to help us sustain our life. However, today we live in a different societal setup than what it used to be in primitive times. So our responses or emotional expressions too have to match our current setup.

Even when we know that, a certain expression of emotion is not an appropriate response or out of proportion, we do not realize that we are losing control when we are taken over by that emotion. Going back to our discussion on how our interpretations of the emotions have a say on the way we express that emotion, will help in understanding why we are unable to control or manage our emotions.

For example, if your neighbor wins one million dollars in a lottery you will be happy, but the intensity of the same emotion would be a lot higher if your neighbor is also your brother or a sister. Clearly, it is all in our head. Who said that we should not feel the same level of excitement for both, but we do not, and we think that it is just normal to feel happier if your sibling wins a lottery when compared to some random neighbor. These are learned frameworks that we continue to follow. Applying the same train of thoughts to negative emotions, they seem to do a lot more harm to us because the response or the expression of a negative emotion is never positive but always negative unless otherwise, one is sadistic or masochistic.

The moral here is that we have enough proofs here that we have choices when it comes how we choose to respond to or express our emotions. It is not a pre-determined, involuntary response or expression. In other words, you have control over your expressions and you certainly cannot pass the buck saying I do not have control over my emotional eating habit. You surely do!

Attachment Styles and Expressing Emotions

The Attachment Styles theory suggests that how we as adults relate with others is strongly influenced by the way we attached ourselves with others as a child. The nature of our interactions with our caregiver forms these attachment styles, which we carry forward to adulthood. According to this theory, there are four styles of attachment namely,

- Secure
- Anxious
- Avoidant and
- Disorganized

Complex studies have been conducted in this field trying to understand the correlation of different attachment styles and the influence these styles have on eating disorders. The term eating disorder covers a larger area and it is not necessarily limited to binge eating. It also includes restrictive eating and other disorders. For our purposes without getting into the technicalities of these complex theories and studies, there could be strong indicators that attachment anxiety is associated with binge eating or emotional eating.

Those who are identified to have attachment anxiety are people who feel insecure when it comes to building intimacy as they are concerned about the possible rejection from the person whom they value or love. They are likely to have poor control over their emotions and boundaries on emotional expressions.

It's All in Your Head

By now you should be able to understand clearly that binge eating is not something that you could change by taking some pills or by taking some herbal supplements. Any recovery and change in the positive direction start with you and what you do with your emotions in your head. Yes, it boils down that 'it's all in your head.'

There are instances whereby people were able to overcome their binge eating issues overnight, but most people had to work it out slowly, living one day at a time. The good news that we have here is that regardless of whether it is overnight or one day at a time, you do not have to be shackled to your old negative responses or eating behaviors. You can decide now in your head to change and can start experiencing the change.

An important key to success here is to get clear on your needs. What is it that you are trying to deal with and how are you going about dealing with it each time you are experiencing a certain emotion? Embrace mindfulness and it will help you keep track of your emotions and your responses. All along, you have been using a specific response to your emotions, which has clearly caused you more harm than good. You now know that you have a choice and an option to choose your responses. Why not choose a response that is useful to you in actually addressing your needs rather than remaining with responses that not only do not meet your needs but also leave you in guilt and in bad shape?

Mindfulness Exercises That You Could Try

You could do several things to remain connected with yourself and practice mindfulness. The internet is inundated with countless suggestions and recommendations on how to remain in a mindful state. You could explore those exercises and pick a few that work for you. Here is a quick reference for you just to help you get started. By no means, these recommendations are exhaustive or comprehensive in any way. Continue exploring your options. What works for one person may not be all that effective for the other person. You need to find your own holy grail until you lock on to strategies that work for you and practice the art of mindfulness.

- Focus on your breath. The idea here is not to control your breath but just to pay attention to your breathing cycles. This is one of the most common mindfulness activity recommended for everyone. You could repeat this as frequently as required throughout the day.

- Pay attention to the task you are engaged in no matter how trivial a task it might be. What exactly are you doing right now? Repeat this during different times of the day and you will be able to realize how mindlessly you engage yourself in various activities.

- Catch your thought, a constant stream of thoughts pass through our minds at unbelievable rates. Hold on for a second and catch your thought, what thought is crossing your mind at this moment. You do not have to control your thought or explore the reasons why you are having such a thought or such thoughts. Just become aware of it briefly and go about continuing your work. Repeat this a few times a day.

Get started with these mindfulness exercises to see how effective they are in helping you become self-aware and mindful. If they work as expected, well and good. If they are not effective for you, do not lose heart find out what works for you because each one is wired differently, and you will certainly be able to find a mindfulness strategy that works the best for you. You may even come up with your own mindfulness techniques and it is not necessary that you have to always take it from an external source.

Chapter 3
Stress and Eating Addiction

The association between stress and overeating has been proven through a number of scientific researches. Therefore, when we talk of stress and eating addiction we are not talking based on anecdotal evidence but on hard scientific facts. How does stress make one overeat and how does that become an addiction?

Can you go back in time when you were enjoying a normal life, a time when you did not have to worry about emotional eating, overweight or obesity? During those times what happened when you were highly stressed? How did you behave in those situations? What exactly did you do? If you could recollect those times when you were healthy, stress did not probably result in addictive eating patterns. If you could recollect further, you will notice that when you were stressed, you were actually not feeling hungry and you would have even skipped meals. You might have been working on your class assignment in the last minute with a close deadline and in those times, you were totally focused on completing your term paper and highly stressed. You would have even forgotten about your food. Even when your parents shouted out for you for the dinner, you screamed back saying you were not hungry... Yes? Are you able to recollect similar situations in the past? I am sure that all of us have many such occasions that we could recollect. Then is it not disproving what we are saying here that stress elicits addictive eating patterns? Are you confused?

Researches indicate that when the stress is of a temporary nature, when it is not of chronic nature, it results in the secretion of epinephrine or what is commonly known as adrenaline. This hormone puts the body into the primitive fight-or-flight response to keep us on the edge and heightens the sensitivity of all our senses to effectively respond to the situation. During these spells of fight-or-flight response, your appetite is put on hold. So when you are stressed you do not feel hungry.

However, the body responds differently when the stress we are talking about is not of a temporary nature. If you are exposed to stressful situations on a daily basis, and if stress becomes the order of the day, your body is programmed to respond differently. Instead of secreting adrenaline, your body will secrete another hormone called cortisol. One of the things the cortisol does is to increase your appetite and increases the motivation to eat. Normally, if the prolonged period of stress disappears the cortisol levels naturally drop down bringing back everything to normal, bringing back your appetite and your motivation to eat to normal levels. On the other hand, if the stressors continue to persist the cortisol levels remain elevated. As long as the cortisol levels remain elevated, so will your appetite levels and your motivation to eat.

Researches also indicate that men and women respond to stress a lot differently. The occurrence of stress-related obesity or overeating patterns is high in women when compared to men.

According to Dr Daryl O'Connor, Lead Researcher at the Leeds University both men and women eat unhealthy food that is high in fat and sugar when they are under prolonged periods of stress at work, but women tend to have greater impact than men.

So the reason why you did not become a victim of stress eating when you were young or when you were healthy was because those stressful episodes were of temporary nature. It is not because you are unhealthy now; you are eating more when stressed, rather you became unhealthy because of overeating that resulted from chronic stress episodes that you are exposed to in your current lifestyle. If you want to do something about your addictive eating pattern, then you must,

1. Do something about the way you respond to stress.

2. Change your lifestyle so that you are not under persistent stress

3. Avoid situations that will not put you under constant stress.

Without doing any of these if you only try to take some pills or change your diet, it is not going to help you in any way. Constantly taking pills to reduce your stress level will only result in other negative side effects. Instead, you should opt for lifestyle changes, which will be more of a natural approach to bringing back your cortisol levels to normal. This will pave way for lasting results and everything else will only produce temporary and unsustainable results.

When does it become an addiction?

There are people who fail to get back to their normal eating habits even after they have made their lifestyle changes and even after they have managed to get their cortisol levels to normal. They continue to have their overeating habits. Why does this happen and how does one then address this situation?

Our body has the tremendous potential to get addicted to things and it could be anything from totally harmless things to something highly harmful. In order to understand this, we need to first understand the addiction cycle.

As far as addiction is concerned, no addiction is developed overnight and the same is true for food addiction. The addiction is developed over a period of time and it could take anywhere between months to years before one reaches the stage of addiction. If one manages to catch the symptoms of addiction early enough and makes the requisite changes, the chances of preventing such addictions are high.

Stage 1: The person is exposed to high levels of stress for a prolonged period resulting in elevated cortisol levels.

Stage 2: As a result, he or she starts overeating. They increase the size of their meal portions and their eating habit becomes more erratic. They do not go by the normal eating cycle rather they feel perpetually hungry and highly motivated to eat. Their consumption and craving for high fat and high sugar food increases.

If they are able to make lifestyle changes in the initial stages of this cycle, they may avert the following disastrous phases.

Stage3: A stage of food tolerance. The body gets used to large portions of food, high fat and high sugar food. During this stage the more they eat the less satisfied they would be. During this stage, they feel the need to increase the food consumption hoping to feel satiated. This results in a vicious cycle.

Stage4: Stage of dependence or addiction. During this stage, the body gets used to consuming so much of calories, high fat food and high sugar food resulting in biological dependence.

Once a person reaches this state of addiction, they need to go through a formal rehabilitation process. However, the term 'addiction' is used very loosely and informally to talk about strong liking towards something. Strong liking towards food in general or a specific type of food is not to be considered an addiction. Rather addiction is a much stronger drive and during this phase the person who is suffering, the addiction does not have any control over their behavior pertaining to the addiction as the biology takes over.

It is therefore important that you closely keep a tab on your own eating habits and if at all any changes to your lifestyle are required, you make them soon instead of waiting for things to get aggravated.

If you are constantly exposed to a high level of stress, it is best to walk out of that situation if it is within your control and if you could afford to pay the price for walking out. At times, you may be working under a difficult boss, putting your life under a very high level of stress but you may not be able to just decide to quit your job one fine morning and walkout of the situation. You may have your bills to pay and other commitments to take care of and in such a situation, you will be forced to present yourself daily without fail to that highly stressful work situation. This is the story of most people. It is only that instead of 'difficult boss' something else will take its place in other people's life. So walking out of the stressful situation is a luxury that many of us do not have. How then should one deal with the situation without subjecting oneself to the risk of landing in food addiction followed by serious health issues?

Remediation and Intervention

If at all one wants to avert the danger of addiction to eating developed out of prolonged episodes of stressful situations, it is important to do something about it as soon as one spots the symptoms of overeating and obesity. Instead of trying to relieve your stress by eating high-fat food and food with high sugar content, which your body is craving for because of the elevated cortisol levels you need to divert your attention to other healthy ways of relieving stress. In the initial stages, it is a lot easier to override the cortisol drive. When things get established, you need to work twice as harder to handle things and to override the cortisol drive.

Avoid being alone

If you had noticed, when you are under stress, loneliness amplifies it. If you happened to have a stressful day, try to visit some friends or go out somewhere with friends. If you come back to your lonely home after a difficult and stressful day you will end up calling your pizza guy and go on an ordering spree. This is not a good way to get rid of stress. If you had a high-stress day, as a rule of thumb be in the crowd.

Pick up a hobby

All of us have hobbies and it does not matter what kind of hobby, as long as it has nothing to do with cooking and food. Getting engaged with your creative hobbies will prove to be a very good stress buster. It could be painting, photography, playing musical instruments, pottery or even if it is just counting the red cars at the traffic signal. Do something you like or rather you love doing, preferably time spent in creating something. You will not only save yourself from being stressed further, but you would have also created something that you could be proud of when you look back.

Sports and Workout

Another good way to overcome the stress is to drain it out by playing a vigorous game or by working out. It has been found that physical exercise helps in secreting four types of happy hormones – Oxytocin, Endorphins, Dopamine and Serotonin. After playing a good game of squash or running around in the basketball field or some rigorous exercise at the gym, you are going to return home happy.

Meditation and Yoga

Meditation and Yoga also have a very positive effect on stress. You will be able to change your mental state from stressful and agitated state to a peaceful and calm state. Instead of waiting for a stressful day to practice Meditation and Yoga, you could make them part of your daily rituals. This will prove to have a very good effect on your mental state. You will also build better resilience to stress and which will prevent you from succumbing easily to stress.

All these remediation and intervention efforts are meant to help you lead a more balanced life. Have a good social life; spend time on yourself and for yourself instead of just making your entire life a work-focused life. All these lubricate your life and keep you generally happy. Try to mix and match the various interventions recommended above. Not everything works the same for everyone; you need to, therefore, find your groove to see what really works for you. There is no hard and fast rule that you need to follow only these things to relieve yourself from stress. You could come up with your own formula of activities that you engage in regularly to relieve stress.

Once you learn to take good care of yourself and be responsible for your own wellbeing, no matter what the external life situations are, you will know how to keep yourself afloat. You do not have control over many things that happen in your life, but you surely do have control over many other things that you could easily change for the better. If you are a victim of stress eating, then you have nothing else and no one else to be blamed but yourself. You just need to make that conscious decision to take good care of yourself, to treat yourself well and be consistent with your efforts.

Chapter 4
Superficial Behaviors – What Should You Do To Stop Them

We have been discussing at great lengths why 'change of diet program' is not the road to recovery when it comes to emotional eating. Your binging is just a symptom and it is not the problem per se. We all know that when it comes to finding a cure to any health issue there is no use treating the symptom rather what is more important and appropriate is dealing with the deeper issues that set the issue in motion. The same is true for binging too. If you are a victim of binging then you should know that you are a victim of some other deeper issue. Try to identify the deeper issues if you want to overcome your binging or overeating issues. Before you identify the underlying issue, you will not be able to get sustainable results. All the efforts you take to overcome your emotional eating issue will be reversed in no time if the source of the problem is not identified and addressed.

In this context, we need to take a look at superficial behaviors. What are these superficial behaviors? Everything that you do that is causing your obesity issue or overweight issue could be classified as superficial behaviors. These are observable behaviors or actions at the top-level. The reality is much deeper, and the problem is not what we see on top and what is observable. Binging or is nothing but the top level behavior or superficial behavior. These superficial behaviors are triggered behaviors or in other words they are responses to something that is happening within you.

If you are leading a highly distracted life, you will have no time to become perceptive of what is happening deep within. You are only going to make a litany of complaints, which are nothing but the observations on the superficial behaviors. These complaints or observations are not going to help you stop the superficial behavior. Your overweight issue will go away only when your superficial behavior changes. However, your superficial behavior will not go away unless and until the source of the problem is addressed.

Instead of running helter-skelter trying to find a quick fix to your binging issues take time to review your life closely. It is not necessary that one should go to a psychologist for counseling or to a psychotherapist. You can be your own therapist if only you train to pay attention to the inner emotions. Step back from the rat race for a moment and transcend to get a bird's eye view of your own life. Observe closely what is happening to you and see where everything is pointing you to and you need to get an even closer. Look at what is happening at the source of all the problems that you are experiencing right now.

Has it to do with any of these following:

- Relationship issue
- Childhood trauma
- Child abuse
- Bullying at school
- Loss of a family member or pet
- Dysfunctional family background

- Failure
- Unemployment
- Insecurity
- Public embarrassment

It may or may not be any of the above and it could be something different or it could be a combination of one or more items in the above list. All these life situations leave a deep scar that is hurting to heal. How you choose to heal those scars is important and among people who suffer from emotional eating issues, it is apparent that they have chosen to overeat as their way to heal those scars.

Being in touch with yourself will go a long way in saving you from getting buried further deep into your problems. Moreover, it will help you understand how you tried to make up for what you were missing in life with food. For example, if you happened to face relationship issues in the past you would be craving for a more intimate and stable relationship. Along the way, you started addressing the craving for a stable relationship through overeating. Now the question is how did food replace those things you were craving for or that you are missing in life? When you ask these vital questions and improve your level of self-awareness in these matters, you are likely to find yourself in a better place when it comes to understanding why it is not possible for you to overcome your binging issues and what is reinforcing the binging behavior.

You need to identify all the components involved so that you can have a complete understanding of the dynamics involved:

1. The superficial behavior – Binging or overeating
2. The underlying cause or deeper issue – What is the deeper

issue in your case?

3. Reinforcement – There is always a reinforcing factor that keeps the loop alive. If it were not for the reinforcement, your superficial behavior would not continue. The reinforcement could be experiencing the pleasure of eating high fat and high sugar food. Or it could be experiencing the sense of satisfaction that you get when you are satiated as you eat huge portions of food. To prolong the feeling of satiation you continue to eat, making you unstoppable.

Identify the above three components to deal with the issue effectively. The dynamics between these three components may not be all that straightforward or evident. At times, it will take time for you to even identify the deeper issue because all along you were thinking that the superficial behavior was the issue and your mind fails to go beyond the superficial issue. You need to patiently work with yourself taking one step at a time until you get the expected breakthrough. A lot of patience is of paramount importance when it comes to dealing with your overeating issues and the associated deeper issue.

Changing Superficial Behaviors: Do I Really Need To Eat That?

When you are on to the pursuit of overcoming your emotional eating or binging issues, you should constantly remind yourself a fact that we have established well in this book. Your eating response is not triggered by the hunger drive. If it were to be driven purely by the hunger drive, your brain's involuntary functions would be set into motion to stop your eating response once you feel satiated. Your brain's signals that tell you are satiated are overridden by the superficial behavior and by the result that you are trying to achieve through that superficial behavior.

If you want to change the superficial behavior, you should start training yourself to listen to your biological signals sent by your brain. If only you had been responding to the brain's signals you would not have reached this spot, where you are now. Even before you start identifying the deeper issues, you could start training yourself on responding to the brain's signals. The point is that when you are binging you really do not have to eat that, so the response to the question, 'Do I really need to eat that?' is a resounding 'NO!' you really do not have to eat that if you are not responding to the hunger drive. You are rather triggered by something else that is totally different from the hunger drive.

What is actually happening above? When you are binging, you are totally distracted and totally engrossed in something else. If only you could stop for a moment and pay attention to what is happening, it would make a whole lot of difference to you. This is where practicing mindfulness becomes very useful. Mindfulness will help you get out of the binging cycle and help you stop the process. Now, this is something that needs to be practiced consciously every time you get into the binging mode. You need to consistently work on breaking the cycle and as frequently as possible. This requires perseverance and patience.

Overcome Difficulties without a Second Helping

Once you understand that your binging is just the superficial behavior, identify the three components that we listed above and learn to break the binging cycle, you will learn to disassociate the superficial behavior from the reinforcing factor, which in turn will help you disassociate food from the deeper issue. You need to understand that whatever emotional difficulties you are experiencing are not related to hunger or food and if that being the case how can you make food the solution to your emotional issues. How do you hope to heal the deep-seated scars with food? This realization has to kick in at some point. All along, you have been making food the solution to your emotional issues and whereas that could never be the solution.

The next time you reach out for your second helping or third helping ask yourself this question, "Is the second helping to satiate my physical hunger?" consciously ask this question every time you go for your second helping or third helping. This conscious question will help you break the pattern.

The truth is that you can overcome your difficulties without a second helping. You might even know this and appreciate greatly what you are reading here. However, when you are actually binging it is like driving in the dark with your headlights switched off. You do not even know what you are getting into, where you are driving and when the road will end. You need to accept these limitations and constantly work on these challenges. The trick here is to leave no exceptions. It does not matter whether you are serving food on to your plate just because you are responding to your hunger drive or it is the kicking in of the binging cycle, ask that vital question you have been given, "Do I really need to eat that?" and tell yourself that your difficulties could be overcome without a second helping. This has to happen over and over until it overrides the negative response to emotions. There can be no holiday to this process because once you slack, the cycle will set in but this time only to come down even more powerfully making it twice harder to overcome. This is where consistency could be put to real use.

Counter Reinforcement

You should set a counter reinforcement to break the reinforcing factor that is at play. You could use several strategies to set this counter reinforcement and put it to work. To start with, you could try to keep track of your eating pattern. Keep a journal for your eating. Put down everything you eat and include as many details as you could, including the frequency at which you are eating. This journal will help you keep track of your food consumption. When you are actually binging you do not realize what you are really eating and how much of it you are consuming. You eat in a thoughtless fashion and you lose control. The idea behind creating a journal is to become mindful of what you are doing. If you are required to make a journal, you need to pay attention to what you are eating, how much you are eating, how many helpings you are taking. Journal sets in the counter reinforcement of mindfulness. If you do this frequent enough, mindfulness will become a part of your eating ritual. Every time you serve food on to your plate your brain will lull you into the mindfulness mode. If you can achieve this state, then it is a partial victory. Everything else will follow soon.

Maintaining a journal is just one of the tools or techniques and you can come up with many such strategies. You could create your own pre-planned menu for every day. Instead of picking something at random you decide in advance what exactly you are going to consume each day and for each meal. Along with it, you could go one step further and keep a very limited supply of food in your pantry. If you have access to unlimited food, you are only facilitating the binging process. On the other hand, if you do not create conditions that support binging then you are likely to reduce the damage caused. Keeping a food journal is to help you reflect on what went on when you were eating. On the other hand, planning your weekly or monthly menu is to decide what is to happen when you go to the table.

Above all try to find some good friends who will support you all through this journey. Someone who is firm with you but also who will be compassionate. This person should be free from any other weaknesses himself or herself, should be a person someone who is psychologically and emotionally strong. Most importantly, this support friend should be a non-judgmental person and someone who will accept you the way you are for who you are and not for what you are.

Chapter 5
Food as Your Solace to Emotional Needs

We have been discussing about emotional eating for a while now. Emotional eating is the response for emotional hunger. We have already seen how emotions such as stress shut down the hunger drive temporarily if the stress is of a temporary nature. On the other hand, if the stress persists a different mechanism is triggered and that sets hunger drive in motion by releasing a stress hormone called cortisol.

Our brain is wired to seek comfort and the drive to seek comfort is much higher when we are under any form of threat. Here, stress is a form of a threat; anything that is unpleasant is considered a threat by the brain. So stress is perceived as a threat. As a result, we seek comfort. This means different things for different people and it depends on how one has been brought up and what kind of childhood experiences they have undergone. All these are set in motion at a much younger age. If you grew up in a safe and secure environment whereby you had a family or someone that you could approach to express your emotions and share your feelings, you would have learned to seek comfort in other people. However, not everyone is lucky to grow up in such a healthy environment. Some people take to some hobbies such as listening to music or playing a musical instrument or something that they will make them feel comfortable. Some do take on to eating as a way to comfort oneself. The pleasurable experience that they have while eating their favorite food makes them experience that sense of comfort. Moreover, the body's drive to reach for high sugar and high fat food becomes high so there is a natural craving for such food when they are trying to comfort themselves, which makes things worse. This will be evident if you observe the eating behavior of people who are emotional eaters. No one goes for salads, greens and sprouts or searches for low fat and low sugar food. Every one of them without any exception (unless they are making a very conscious decision every time not to go for such items) goes for high fat and high calorie food when they go on a binge-eating spree.

We cannot run away from any of our emotions and it is not practical to run away from them. If we try to run away from our emotions, we would only be living in denial. Emotions are not bad, and we need these emotions to feel alive. However, how one copes with their emotions is important and it decides whether we went around as healthy people or have a secret life where we hide food in all sorts of places and eat secretly and rapidly whenever you go through any of these emotions that trigger your binge eating pattern.

So how do you cope with your emotion and is food your comforter when you are upset, stressed, depressed, afraid or suffering any such emotions? Pay attention to what happens when you are binging. Do you feel relieved when you stuff your mouth with loads of your favorite high fat food? After gobbling rapidly, do you breathe a sigh of relief? Just paying attention to your own responses and your interaction with food it will shed you so much light on the dynamics involved. We are often unable to change the situation for better just because we do not understand what is happening. We do not understand what is happening because we are not stopping for a moment to pay attention to things. The first step to recovery as we keep reiterating is focus and mindfulness. However, mindfulness alone is not enough to change things, but it certainly aids recovery along with the other appropriate interventions.

What Is Nervous Hunger?

Nervous hunger – this is nothing, but the games played by the hormones. Our biology is wired to survive. Whenever a threat is sensed, the word threat has as many interpretations as there are people. Nervousness or anxiety could be seen as a threat by the brain and our biology responds in a preset way once the threat is sensed. As a result, it does everything to increases the chances of survival. The temporary shutting down of hunger is to let the body focus on the immediate fight-or-flight response, which is supposed to help in surviving the threat. In case the threat continues to persist it prepares the body further to survive by increasing the craving for high fat and high sugar food so that one may have adequate energy to fight the threat that one is faced with. This is a natural process; however, one reaches the binging stage if they have not developed other healthier coping mechanisms. The question is whether it is possible to control nervous hunger so that we can save ourselves from becoming a victim of binge eating.

Is It Possible To Control Nervous Hunger?

The answer to the above question is both 'yes' and 'no'. Without understanding and accepting your situation without denying, explaining away or giving excuses, it is not possible to control nervous hunger. If you want to change things for the better here and break out of the habit, then start with 'acceptance', your mantra for healing and recovery.

When you are binging as a result of nervousness you are sucked into a vicious cycle of Signal – Desire to Eat – Gratification – Habit. We have already seen how this vicious cycle is initiated by the biology and how it is kept in motion by habit formation, dependency and addiction. Let us look at the key steps in breaking away from this vicious cycle.

Step 1 – Awareness

Increasing your level of awareness is a prerequisite here and without which you are not going to move any further. Every time you reach out for food regardless of the triggering factor, stop for a moment to ask yourself whether you are going to eat now as a way of comforting yourself or are you responding to your hunger drive. Things will tend to slow down a bit once you stop for a moment to ask this basic question, even if it does not immediately change things. If you have already developed a habit and moved to the state of dependency on excess eating, then it will take time for you to break away from this habit and mere awareness is not the solution. You need to take a realistic approach when you are trying to recover and not develop false hope. If anyone is going to tell you that all you need to do to change this is to become aware then you should know that it is time to walk away from such a strategy or person who recommends awareness as the 'be all and end all solution' to recovery from binge eating.

Step 2 – Build a New Habit

When you are trying to overcome binge eating you are trying to overcome your old habits. It is much easier to change the behavior by forming a new habit in place of the old one instead of just trying to stop the old behavior. The goal here is to replace the old negative behavior with a new positive or at least neutral behavior. It is important that you mustn't replace one negative behavior with another negative behavior.

Remember the forming of any new habit will have its own cycle and take its own time. You cannot form a habit overnight. It is with repetition we form habits and that is how you formed your previous negative habit. So do not be unrealistic with your expectations. You need to consistently work on forming another new, positive habit.

When you were going through a binge eating episode every time you felt nervous, distressed, sad, stressed or feeling any other such emotion you were trying to comfort yourself as you had sometime in the past learned this behavior which developed into a habit. If you want to change this negative habit with a new positive habit, you should rewire the entire system so that you feel comforted by repeating the new behavior every time you go through those emotional spells.

While building your new positive behavior try to keep things simple. The new behavior should be pleasurable in some way so that you are motivated to embrace it. In case of eating, you were able to so easily get hooked on to this behavior because your brain is naturally wired to see food and eating as pleasurable acts and that is why it triggers the reward pathway every time you eat. This is the brain's way of motivating you to repeat this behavior as it is an essential act of survival when you are responding to natural hunger drive. If your brain does not trigger the reward pathway each time you eat, you will not do anything even something as much as moving your little finger when you feel hungry and thereby end up perishing. Each time you feel hungry you should go hunting for food as in the primitive days, cook food or drive to a restaurant or at least order food from your local takeaway. All these are important acts of survival. That is why it was so easy for food to become an addiction.

Similarly, when you are setting a new habit in place of the old one, it is important to find something that is easy to take on, pleasurable in some way so that your brain will support your new habit formation by triggering the reward pathway to motivate you to repeat such a behavior every time you are nervous.

Step 3 – Organize

It is much easier to break away from the emotional eating habits or nervous hunger cycle with a bit of organization. One of the things that you should do is to create a timetable for all your meals and schedule it to the last detail. This schedule or timetable will teach your brain to stimulate the hormonal secretion that is responsible for hunger drive only during those scheduled times. This will enable you to gain better control over your eating habits. It does not matter whether you are hungry or emotionally charged, the best way of disassociating the emotions and the eating response is to stick to scheduled eating. This is yet another habit formation. Stay away from food at other unscheduled times. Initially, you are likely to lapse several times but when you have a schedule to follow you will at least create a mental marker that you are faltering each time you are eating at unscheduled times and over a period you will be able to adhere to your schedule.

Further to that, try to schedule your entire day instead of just the meal times. Organizing your entire day will bring some discipline into your life and it will further enhance your self-control skills.

Step 4 – Diet

Remember, just as we are trying to break away from the vicious cycle of nervous eating responses, try to pay attention to your diet as well. Try to replace high fat food and high sugar food with more healthy food so that you will gradually be able to work on your weight as well. Eating healthy will save you from feeling guilty and it will also contribute to your overall, general wellbeing. This sense of wellbeing is important for anyone that is trying to recover from binge eating or emotional eating.

Binge eating destroys your sense of wellbeing, making you feel miserable about yourself. Whenever you feel miserable, you will be looking for comfort. As you have already established a pattern of finding comfort in food, you will quickly regress to your old negative habits. If you want to avoid getting back to that rut over and over you need to start feeling good about yourself and this will happen when you start eating healthy. A well-balanced diet will trigger happy hormones and help you stay emotionally healthy too. So focus on a good, well-balanced diet that you could follow during the scheduled meal times.

Step 6 – The Sponsor or Support Network

Who said that you need to fight it out all by yourself? If that is what you have been believing all along then it is time to break away from such beliefs. Do not stress yourself with this thought rather open up to the support network, to people who really care about you and your wellbeing. It could be anyone from your immediate family members, friends or even a colleague. Try to find such a person or a group that will support you in your journey. The chances of lapsing are many and you should not be deterred completely just because you have lapsed from your efforts. If you have a sponsor who is ready to support you in times of such setbacks, motivate you, cheer you and get you back on track, the chances of success are high when compared to someone who is doing it all by oneself without anyone to support them. When you have a sponsor, you will feel accountable for your setbacks.

This will go a long way in helping you keep on track. Make sure that you find a person or a group that will is genuinely concerned about you and genuinely care about you. If you do not have anyone that you could count on then it is best to seek professional assistance such as working with a coach whom you meet regularly.

Often we are too harsh on ourselves and it is certainly not a productive behavior. Being harsh on yourself will only build unnecessary resistance and you will end up achieving just the opposite of what you want to achieve. It is certainly possible to break away from the vicious cycle of nervous eating. Be kind to yourself and allow yourself enough time to respond to the new efforts you are making on your road to recovery.

Chapter 6
Hunger, Belly, Brain

The brain controls our body and its functions. Our brain constantly sends signals to different parts of the body to perform certain functions and respond in a certain way. Most of these responses result in the secretion of different types of chemicals that make us experience different emotions.

We receive the stimulus or the triggers from the external world and our brain processes that information and sets a series of processes in motion that make us feel happy, sad, stressed, and anxious and experience other such emotions. We are controlled by these emotions and the chemicals that are produced in our body.

Another important factor to note here is that the human gut has a direct hotline to the brain, and it uses a series of hormones to communicate with the brain. It has also been found that the human gut consists of 100 million neurons and neurons are the stuff that our human brain is made of and we have over 100 billion neurons in the brain. In a way, our stomach is our second brain. Not only that, our stomach has exclusive pathways that interact with the brain stem.

What do all these bits and pieces of information mean in the context of what we are discussing here – the emotional hunger? It simply means that our stomach has a lot more influence on our entire system than we could possibly think of.

What happens when you feel hungry? This is how the process goes. When your stomach is empty, it connects with your brain through those exclusive pathways indicating that something needs to be done about it. This is how the hunger pang is felt and we respond to this hunger drive. When we eat responding to food, our brain triggers another circuit called the reward pathway. When this pathway is triggered, it releases the feel-good hormones called the dopamine. This is a motivator hormone that encourages you to repeat this behavior. This is a survival strategy, which the brain has been using for millions of years.

There is yet another piece of information that might be useful in understanding why we tend to overeat. Normally once we start consuming food, we should feel full and feel satiated. This should send further signals to the brain that reduces the drive to eat. This brings the eating process to a halt only to be repeated when your energy resources run down again. However, our brain is also designed to preserve us, and it always runs under the presumption 'What if the body runs out of energy and we do not get food at that time?' and it allows the signals of satiation to be overridden allowing us to continue eating even when we are feeling full. Or, in other words, the sense of 'feeling full' is numbed and we go on an eating spree or eat without stopping.

Understanding all these dynamics help us have better control over our eating habits. There is always a constant dialogue going on between our brain and the belly and vice versa. Everything, therefore, depends on what our brains tell the belly and what the belly, in turn, tells the brain.

Emotions and Bodily Sensations

Have you ever stepped on to a stage to give a short speech? Before giving the speech what was your emotional state? If this were to be your first time facing a public speaking situation, then you are likely to be tensed and anxious or even afraid. All these are considered negative emotions even though inherently they all have their own positive intended outcome, which is to protect you from the impending threatful situation.

While anticipating the public speaking situation if you had paid attention to your bodily sensations which you would not have done at that time anyway, you would have experienced an uncomfortable feeling in your stomach which is often expressed as butterflies in the stomach. This is one of the most situations that we could present whereby an emotional state triggers a specific bodily sensation. Each one would have their own way of responding to these emotional states. What is to be noted here is that there is always an associated bodily sensation whenever you experienced an emotional state. This is applicable not only for the so-called negative emotions but also for the positive emotions.

Your Body – Feelings and Sensations

When you are trying to overcome your negative response patterns associated with eating, it is important that you learn to pay attention to the emotions and the associated sensations so that you could learn to disassociate yourself with those sensations to overcome the obsessive behavior. Here is a quick exercise to train yourself to pay attention to the various sensations in your body. We are going to follow an exercise from the Indian Yoga tradition, and it is called 'savasana', which translates to 'corpse pose', a meditative yoga posture that helps in relaxation and rejuvenation of the body. We are going to use this technique to train your mind to pay attention to the sensations in different parts of your body.

This could be done by either sitting or lying down. You should, however, find a quiet place where you are not likely to be disturbed by other unnecessary noises or people. It is not necessary that there has to be pin-drop silence, but avoiding unnecessary distractions will help you reach deeper states.

Take the most comfortable posture either sitting down or lying down. If you are lying down face the palm downwards. Pay attention to all the sounds around you and as you hear the sounds, you traverse into deeper states of relaxation. As you are feeling relaxed, take a nice deep breath. Imagine your breath filling your entire body as you breathe in and slowly breathe out imagining the air from all the parts of the body slowly being released from all the parts of the body from toe to head. Repeat this breathing cycle twice more. After that, take a deep breath and this time focus on the individual parts of the body starting from the toe and move upward. Make sure that you focus on the right to separately and left toe separately and this applies to the limbs. Imagine the air filling in the part that you are focusing when you breathe in and the air being released out of that part when you breathe out. As you are doing, this pays attention to the associated sensation in each part. Pay attention to contrasts in the sensations as you keep moving around from one part to the other. Just pay attention to the sensation and no further effort is required from your part. Once you have covered all the parts of the body from your toes to the tip of your hair, gently take a deep breath and breathe out to gently return to the natural state while still feeling relaxed.

Repeat the above process a few more times and this will make you adept in noticing fast the bodily sensations.

Your Body Image

The image that we have about our own body is not something that we change on a daily or monthly basis. This is a deeply ingrained image that is shaped over the years.

You could have,

- a positive or healthy body image
- negative body image
- have a neutral body image

Regardless of whatever image you hold about your body, you should know that these images are not formed overnight. It took several years for you to form the image that you hold in your head through the interplay of several factors.

Every emotional state has an associated physical response as in the case of fear and anxiety associated with public speaking causing the discomfort in the tummy.

If you go through a series of positive experiences, you are likely to experience positive physical response. Then you are likely to build a positive image of your body because that is what you remember - positive or pleasant physical experiences.

In your childhood, if you have been going through a series of negative experiences then your body would have been experiencing a series of negative responses, discomfort in different parts of your body. Over a period these negative physical state is what you remember whenever you think of your body. In effect, you are likely to consider your body as a burden or as something negative.

As you grow up, the image you hold in your head will control who you are and how you behave in different situations. This paves way for unhealthy eating habits and binging. If you hold a negative image of your body, then you could be seeking relief through food. Dieting is such cases is not going to help you resolve the issue. You will continue to have these issues even if you experience temporary success with your diet plan.

Early Parental Relationship, Attachment Styles and Your Body Image

Your relationship with your parents or your guardians or with people who had control over your life has a lot to do with your body image. If you grew up in a healthy and fully functional family with a happy childhood, you will be in a position to trust adults. You will be able to express your emotions and seek their support whenever you needed their support. If you had unwelcoming adults who were dismissive of your feelings and emotions, then you learn not to trust them, and you tend to become an independent person. In this case, you are building yourself as an independent person as a defense mechanism and this is different from that of the healthy sense of independence. When the sense of independence is built as a defense mechanism then you would be unable to get into any serious relationship and you will not be able to build lasting emotional bonding with anyone and not necessarily with adults. This will, in turn, affect your social life.

The danger here is that you may take on to an avoidant attitude, which spreads through all aspects of your life. So much so you get disconnected with your own emotions and the associated body sensations. This attachment style is referred to as the avoidant attachment.

'Emotion – Body Sensation' connect is a very important mechanism to stay healthy both mentally and physically. When you turn numb to this connection, you may fail to take notice of the signals your body is sending to your brain about your hunger drive or the sense of satiation when you are full while eating a meal. This could eventually result in habitual overeating issues. Under normal circumstances, while eating, once the stomach is full the stomach signals the brain to stop eating. If you have trained yourself to ignore these signals through avoidant attitude and the associated negative body image created by a series of negative childhood experiences, then you do not stop eating even after feeling full.

What needs to be understood here is that you cannot go back and change your parental relationship or your experiences. However, it is possible to change your current response to food and hunger. Just because you have developed an avoidant attitude to pay attention to your body sensations it does not mean that is the only way to respond to current situations too by holding on to strategies and responses that were not essentially useful today. You have the freedom to respond differently and to train yourself to respond differently in such a way that the new response is useful to you at all levels.

In case you have had a parent or a guardian who has been highly inconsistent then you could end up with ambivalent attachment. As it happens in a number of cases, sometimes the parents or the guardians would be too caring and super good taking care of all their kid's needs both spoken and unspoken. They would shower their kids with love and make themselves fully available to their kids, listen to them and make them experience that their emotions do matter, and they are important. At other times, the same parents would exhibit just diametrically opposite behavior. They will not be available to meet the needs of the kids, engrossed in their own world and would not want to be disturbed. They will get angry and annoyed when approached. They will also make their kid experience that his or her feelings are not important. A child that grows up in this inconsistent environment does not know what to expect from the adults. He or she will have issues trusting adults and when they grow up, they will have issues trusting others in general because they are not sure how the other person will behave the next moment. They do not want to feel let down or neglected so they will avoid building strong bonds or make themselves available for any kind of relationship. This ambivalent attachment could also force one to find consolation in food.

Children who grow up in an abusive environment or unsafe environment could end up developing disorganized attachment. As it happens in the case of

- dysfunctional families
- a family whereby a parent is addicted to alcohol or other addictive substances
- emotionally imbalanced
- a physically ill parent who had to be taken care of by the child

In all the above or similar situations the child that is supposed to get the care and attention of the parent fails to get the required attention and care. Instead, he or she is subjected to distressing and a series of unpleasant experiences. Not only that in case of a physically ill parent, the child ends up taking care of the parent besides not getting the care and attention that they are supposed to be getting them from adults. As they grow up in such an environment, they learn to disconnect themselves from their own emotions. They tend to disqualify their own emotional needs because they feel that it did not matter. As an adult when such children think of their childhood all that they have is nothing but a stressful moment and every time they think of their childhood they feel stressed. Even though they tend to ignore their emotional state at the intellectual level, their body exhibits the responses that are associated with the emotional state. This, in turn, triggers the stress eating symptoms. Even if this person is currently not in any stressful moment, they live in a perpetually stressful state because of the strong images of the stressful childhood that they hold in their head. Our brain is good at simulating the stress even when there are no triggers in the present day but based on past experiences. Our brain's goal is to protect the self from perishing so it keeps the body prepared and protected from situations that could possibly lead to those threats of the past. All these create a vicious stress eating cycle.

Despite having any of the above negative attachment styles, one may not necessarily end up having a negative body image or the associated negative eating responses. However, what needs to be taken into consideration is the fact that someone with such negative attachment style is more prone to eating disorders and overeating issues when they are subjected to stress. This also does not mean someone who does not have any of these negative attachment styles would always deal with stress or other emotions in a healthy way. Even as an adult one could learn or take on to the negative eating responses leading to overeating and emotional eating patterns. It is easier to deal with the issues when you know the underlying currents. People who fail to address the underlying current but try one diet program after the other hoping to reduce weight end up failing in their attempts to control their eating patterns and the associated overweight issues.

When you understand your attachment style and the resulting behavior, you have a chance to manage the behavior, change your responses and reclaim a healthy lifestyle with healthy eating habits.

Establishing Mindful Relationship with Food by keeping a Tab on Body Sensations

One of the best ways to control your eating behavior is by keeping a tab on your body sensations. We have already noted that every emotional state triggers a specific set of physical sensations in the body. We are trying to reverse engineer the whole process. Your physical sensations could help you become mindful and be aware of what is happening 'at the moment'.

If you could step back and observe what is happening, all your emotional states are not because of what is happening in the present moment. They either have something to do with the past happenings or your future fears or apprehensions. What is connecting your past or future and your present is your body and that is where you experience everything? There cannot be a better way to get started with controlling your behavior or managing your behavior with respect to overeating or binging.

We have already gone through the exercise on how to train your body to pay attention to the body sensations in this chapter. The more perceptive you become of your body sensations the higher the level of mindfulness. In the earlier chapters, we have already seen how mindfulness will aid in gaining better control over our eating responses and binging.

The easiest and in fact the best way to keep a tab on your body sensations is to ask a simple question, "How am I feeling right now?" The words "right now" are the grounding words that bring you to the present where exactly your body is, and it will set a series of the process required for reaching the state of mindfulness.

Our ability to remember the past should serve a better purpose – hold on to the good memories of your past that will trigger a positive emotional state. Similarly, the ability to think about the future should serve a better purpose too – visualize yourself emerging successfully from the situation that you are considering a threat and walk back one step at a time to see what needs to happen for you to emerge successfully; invest your time and focus your attention on planning for success. This way, your past and future could serve you to feel good and do better.

Body Disconnection and Obsession

One of the important factors to pay attention to in the discussion on the attachment style is that one could disconnect oneself from one's body psychologically if they happen to have a negative attachment type. When you feel a sense of disconnect from your body, then you are also going to ignore the body sensations. If you ignore the body sensations, then you are going to ignore the signals your brain sends while you are eating, and you will not be able to stop even when you feel satiated. It is therefore important to establish the 'connect' with your body.

It does not even occur to us that we could have a sense of disconnect with our body. It is difficult to perceive such a state for most of us. Here are a few indicators that you could be in the state of disconnect with your body.

For example,

- Do you often feel that you are in a different location than the real location in which you are living?

- Do you feel that the things around you and the world around you are unreal?

- Do you experience the happenings of your daily life as an outsider watching a movie?

Many of us have such experiences from time to time. However, if this experience is going to persist for a long span of time or if that is your regular state then it is likely that you are having dissociative disorders. A strong link has been found between people with obsession and dissociative disorder. If you are feeling disconnected from your body and you also have emotional eating issues, then it is best that you talk to a counselor or a therapist to have this condition addressed rather than trying to change your diet plans with the intention of addressing your overeating issues.

What Effect does Trauma Have on Your Relationship with Your Body?

Traumatic experiences whether it is an accident, physical abuse either sex or violence, loss of a loved one, etc., tend to leave its scars as 'body memory' as opposed to conscious memory. If people who have gone through these traumatic experiences are unable to talk about those experiences or if they are even unable to remember what exactly happened because your brain has stored the information in a different format and that is why they find it difficult to recollect the details of the traumatic experience.

When the senses are presented with the sensory stimulus that was originally associated with a traumatic experience, the individual is likely to set the bad memories in motion and the individual is likely to experience things as if they are happening in the present moment being unable to control one's feelings of fear, stress or even anger. They try to calm down their emotions in different ways and some people take to eating as a way of calming oneself down. This presents a clear case for stress eating. The stress has nothing to do with what is happening here and now, but it is triggered by a smell or a sound or a specific visual input that was originally associated with the traumatic experience. People who have undergone traumatic experiences in the past are likely to be extra vigilant about things around them. This takes the toll out of them as they are under the constant stress of having to be alert 24x7. At times, they may not even have a sound sleep. In an effort to feel normal such people look for external stimulus to feel in control of the situation, which in turn leads to behaviors such as overeating or substance abuse or sex.

If you want to change things for the better, then the best place to get started is your own body. Start listening to your body, it is constantly sending out loads of signals and if only you could pay attention to those signals and respond to them appropriately you are likely to save yourself from most of the issues pertaining to overeating and binging.

Learn to work with your body rather than considering it as an adversary or as an issue to be dealt with. You have never had control over your past and you never will. The same applies to your future as well. All that you have is your present moment and your body to work with. Getting started with your body now by paying attention to the body sensations and being mindful of your experiences every moment will go a long way in overcoming your overeating issues and binging.

Chapter 7
Eating Disorders

An eating disorder is where a person who suffers this condition exhibits abnormal eating behaviors that affect one's health. It also affects one's emotional life making it impossible for them to function normally taking care of their day-to-day activities.

There are three types of eating disorders:

- Anorexia Nervosa
- Bulimia Nervosa and
- Binge Eating disorder

These eating disorders could show up at any age. However, the most common age groups associated with these disorders are teenage and young adulthood.

Anorexia Nervosa

The person who suffers from Anorexia Nervosa is someone who entertains abnormal fear of overweight and overcautious about gaining weight. Owning to their fear of gaining weight, they go to unbelievable extents to reduce their weight. People with this eating disorder will actually have alarmingly low weight but they will continue to diet to lose further weight, so much so they even turn weak and anemic, resulting in health issues. These people literally count their calories. They try to use unnatural methods to reduce their weight. One of the common traits to be noticed among these people is vomiting after every meal. In extreme cases, they even go to the extent of starving themselves under the pretext of dieting and fasting.

Dieting and fasting are healthy practices and millions of people follow these practices, but in the case of someone who suffers, Anorexia Nervosa is that they take things to the extremes.

Despite their thin appearance, they will have a distorted image of their body, and they see themselves fat as opposed to reality. Statistics have that people who suffer this eating disorder have the highest mortality rate among the other mental disorders. Health complications of this eating disorder range from constipation, low blood pressure, organ failure to brain damage.

Bulimia Nervosa

Bulimia Nervosa is the opposite condition of Anorexia Nervosa. Those who suffer from Bulimia Nervosa are people who eat abnormally large quantities of food at frequent intervals. If people with Anorexia Nervosa are thin and anemic, these people will be obese. They go on to overeating spree or what is called binge eating.

Interestingly, even those who suffer Bulimia Nervosa are concerned about their body weight like in the case of Anorexia Nervosa. They use compensatory techniques including but not limited to induced-vomiting after eating, use of laxatives, fasting and workouts. They exhibit a lack of control over their eating habit. These people suffer health conditions like high blood pressure, diabetes, severe gastrointestinal issues, besides several others.

Binge Eating Disorder

Binge Eating Disorder is also signified by overeating issues like that of Bulimia Nervosa. Here again, the one who suffers this disorder does not have control over the food. They consume abnormally large portions of food at frequent intervals. The only difference between the one who suffers Bulimia Nervosa and Binge Eating Disorder is that these people do not use any compensatory techniques such as induced vomiting or the use of any laxatives or other such artificial methods to lose weight.

One of the questions that perplexes the healthcare industry is why do people exhibit such eating disorders. The reasons or the causes are not that easy to explain. There is always more than one reason or cause why a person suffers from a particular eating disorder ranging from hereditary reasons, sociological reasons, and psychological reasons to hormonal imbalance. A complex set of dynamics is established among the one or more factors and the combination of these causes that results in a specific disorder in an individual varies from a person to person. If one is not able to overcome their overweight issue or obesity issue with dieting and a good workout schedule, then you should know that the root cause of the disorder is not addressed. The solution or the recovery to these disorders often involves multiple disciplines – psychotherapy, counseling, medical attention, nutrition planning, dieting and workout plans. Only when a holistic approach is taken it is possible to overcome the issues or else the results obtained will only be of temporary nature. Unless and otherwise a holistic approach is taken, all the efforts will only produce superficial results.

Along with all the other efforts, the person who is trying to recover from any of these disorders should design a healthy, well-balanced lifestyle. They will also need the support of their family and friends. It will take a considerable amount of time for them to regain their lost self-esteem. This is where the moral support of the family and friends would prove to be highly beneficial.

Chapter 8
The Friend You Need The Most Now is YOU

All of us have those voices in our heads that control our behaviors. We cannot switch off these voices and they have the capacity to put us through a real rollercoaster experience. Even though these are the voices in our heads, they are actually not our own voices.

The voices that we hear in our head are voices that we internalized and made them our own as we grew up. The nature of the voices that we hear could be grouped into three categories:

1. Supportive and self-assuring voice

2. Critical and judgmental voice

3. Neutral voice that states the facts and presents an objective view

Depending on the context, the nature of these voices changes. All of us are capable of hearing all three voices. However, there is always a dominant voice that determines our approach to life and how we end up handling things. These voices are meant to be helpful to us, but they are not always as helpful as they are supposed to be. Often, they turn out to be unproductive.

When you are trying to overcome your overeating issues or

your binge eating issues, don't you think that it would be really nice to have a shoulder to lean on to, a friend who is non-judgmental and someone who will just accept us the way we are? However, not everyone is lucky enough to have such a friend or a family member.

You actually do not have to look for such a friend or a support elsewhere, outside you. This friend and support is just inside you - your inner voice. Remember we spoke just a while ago about the three types of voices in our head, it is time to gain access to that supportive and self-assuring voice that is inside you, which always keeps telling you that it is possible, and you can do it. You have already experienced the power of this voice on many occasions in your life and you just need to tap the potential of that voice and that friend within you. Yes, the friend that you need the most now is YOU!

Listen to the self-nurturing voice in you! Work consistently to strengthen that voice. Gain access to that loving and supporting self that is in you for comforting words each time you are distressed and each time you feel weak. No matter how bleak the situation is, and no matter how wasted you think you are at the moment, this self-nurturing voice is very much alive within you. It is useful to believe in the power of this voice than looking for external support. This is not to mean that you should close yourself to the external support that you could possibly get. It is important to get all the help you could. However, there is no guarantee that the external support will be there always, whenever you need it. What you can be sure of is your own inner self-nurturing voice. You cannot run away from that voice and that voice cannot run away from you either. Reinforce this alliance that you already have and continue offering yourself the love, support and the comfort that you need as you journey towards your recovery.

Here are a few things that you could do to reinforce the alliance.

1. Assure yourself that you have that loving self-nurturing support within you by saying something like. "I am here to support you, no matter what! You are not alone!"

2. Let the inner voice speak to you using comforting words along these lines, "You are doing great and you are going to pull it off!"

3. Let your comforting words be accompanied by comforting and self-assuring gestures as if your friend is using those gestures on you.

Reframing Self-Defeating Thoughts

One of the most important steps in this journey is reframing of those self-defeating thoughts. No matter how strong the inner nurturing voice is and no matter how good a friend that we try to be to ourselves, from time to time these self-defeating thoughts will emerge just in those moments of weakness trying to undo everything that we have been working towards all along. If at all, you want to be successful with your efforts you need to make sure that you catch these self-defeating thoughts that try to nullify all your efforts and change them to self-empowering thoughts.

For example, you could be telling yourself, "No matter how hard I try, I always fail!" There could be so many different variations of this self-defeating thought, but the bottom line is this. The self-defeating thought reminds you of your impending failure. Such thoughts are based on exaggerated truths.

It might be true that you have failed in the past with some of your efforts despite making the required efforts. The self-defeating thought tries to absolutize this and tries to convince you saying that you will always fail. Just because you have failed in the past, it does not mean you will always fail. You need to spot such flaws in the self-defeating thought. All that it takes is to ask a simple question, "Have I never been successful in my life?" The answer is going to be "No!"

List all those times that you were successful with your efforts no matter how small the effort or achievement is, for now even the smallest of those achievements are here to prove to you that the self-defeating thought is incorrect, and you do not have to go by it any longer.

Reframe the self-defeating thought to an empowering thought looking at your own proofs from your past:

"When I make consistent efforts I succeed."

"I have succeeded in the past and I know I will succeed in this too, it is a matter of time!"

"I am successful with my efforts today!"

Repeating these self-empowering thoughts whenever the self-defeating thought pops up will help you stay focused.

What Are The Resources To Which You Have Access?

No matter how bleak the situation may turn out to be as opposed to what most of us tend to think or believe, we are not left without any resources. We certainly do have access to several resources that we could use to overcome the challenges that we face. These resources can be categorized into three groups as follows:

1.   **Internal Resources** – There isn't a single person that comes without these Internal Resources. The nature and the range of these internal resources may vary from person to person,

but we all possess an amazing set of internal resources. To give a few examples – perseverance, resilience, high energy, courage and patience besides countless others.

2. **External Resources** – As social beings, we have access to numerous external resources that we have access to and that we could use. Examples of external resources include – Family, friends, spouse, therapy or counseling, religion and so on.

3. **Survival Resources** – These are childhood strategies that we used to adapt to a challenging situation when we are young. These are often driven by our instincts with the intention of protecting us. These survival resources may or may not be useful as adults. As a young kid, we might run away from the spot when we are bullied at school. However, as an adult, this survival resource may not be that useful as it can damage our self-image and self-esteem. Alternatively, we would want to confront the situation boldly, which is likely to meet the purpose or solve the issue at hand better. When you are assessing your own survival resources, you need to use your discretion, as they could be nothing but a primitive survival response.

When you are on your road to recovery, trying to combat the challenges in overcoming your emotional eating issues, it would be highly useful to pool in all the resources that you could possibly access regardless of whether it is internal, external or survival. Most often, we do not even acknowledge that we have access to these resources. We conveniently ignore the fact that we could tap these resources and find it easy to believe that your situation is helpless. Remember, you are not in a helpless situation no matter how worse it looks. You just need to know where to look for this help. The very act of listing all the resources that you have access to will give you a great sense of hope. You will be able to devise your own winning combinations of these resources to deal with the issues. What might have looked completely hopeless, in light of these resources would turn hopeful.

Take Care of Your Needs and Set the Limits

If you had paid close attention to the whole dynamics involved in your emotional eating issues, everything revolves around addressing your needs. However, the strategies that you have been using to take care of your needs are faulty. Instead of taking care of your needs by addressing the underlying cause of the need, you have been treating the symptoms and in the process you have ignored the real issues for long enough for it to create new issues in your life. Instead, by practicing mindfulness and by paying attention to your body sensations you will be able to get to the core of the issues and address the actual needs. When this happens, there will be no need to seek solace in food.

You do not have to look for the solutions in other things or in other people. Everything you need to feel complete is within you.

Setting the Limits

Setting nurturing limits is one of the crucial steps in the recovery process. You would have tried hard all along to stop your binge eating issue but one area where most people fail is to do with setting limits. Either you would have absolutely no limit or you would have been too harsh with yourself in setting highly restrictive limits. Both the approaches are not useful because,

1. When you set no limits, you do not have any mental marker to tell you when to stop. As a result, you continue with your binging ignoring the brain's signals when you feel full.

2. When you set highly restrictive limits on yourself, the effectiveness is very limited because you would only be setting in motion a very high level of resistance. Within no time, you would

be out of your diet program or rigorous workout plan.

On the contrary, you need to set nurturing limits. Remember, the friend that you need the most is YOU. Set limits that are easy to adhere to so that you will not feel restricted but encouraged to follow. You can keep stretching these limits with time without eliciting internal resistance.

For instance, if you feel like enjoying your favorite chocolate brownie after a stressful day, instead of saying no to your desire and limiting yourself from completely avoiding the chocolate brownie, decide in advance that you will limit with just a single chocolate brownie. When you drive to your local confectionery to buy your brownie, just pick one and drive back. Do not test your will power at this stage and it is totally unnecessary to put your will power to test at this point of time.

If you have been having a chocolate brownie every day set the limit to two chocolate brownies per week. When you are setting these limits, the whole point is to have control over the entire eating response and not to deprive yourself of the simple harmless pleasures of life and chocolate brownies are one such harmless simple pleasures of life that you are entitled to but it becomes a problem only when you gobble half a dozen of them in a single sitting.

Setting such nurturing limits with every meal, with your shopping budget and with the frequency at which you eat, will set in motion a series of internal process, which will eventually help you gain more control over the entire binge eating process. Along with it, if you could club that most important question, "Do I really need to eat that?" every time you feel like eating when you are not really feeling hungry will change things for the better.

In all these, you need to be extremely patient with yourself.

Remember your emotional eating habit is not something that developed overnight. It took you so many weeks and months to be where you are now. Expecting this response to change overnight would be an unrealistic expectation. Allow yourself enough time and if you happen to fail along the way, let that self-assuring and nurturing voice talk to you saying, just because you have failed once it does not mean that you will never succeed. Pick up where you left off and continue.

Chapter 9
Finding Your True Self

We are living in a fast-paced world, all of us are running frantically hoping to find what we want, and in the process, we lose our true self in this rat race. We do not even know after a certain point of time that why we are running; despite that, we cannot stop running because of the fear that if we stop running others will overtake us and we will be left behind. For the modern mind, this is something indigestible and something that we cannot take.

As we grow up, we grow up with our dreams and aspirations that are in alignment with our true self. When we lose ourselves in the rat race, we forget these dreams and aspirations too, but it does not mean that they have disappeared or ever. Unless and until we respond to that call and to that vocation, we can never be our true self. Even if it looks that we are winning and living the life everyone envies, we will feel a lacuna, a great gulf, a sense of emptiness. Only when we get connected with our original call and respond to that call will, we be able to understand and be who we really are.

It is not possible to get connected with our true self and to respond to the call to be who we really are unless and until we stop for a moment, go to that still space within and listen.

Losing our true self is the modern-day curse. It is high time that you established a connection with your true self when you are trying to overcome your binge eating issues. The inner lacuna and the sense of emptiness could be what you have been trying to fill with your emotional eating behavior. You could be trying to find that true self through food; hardly has anyone managed to reach their true self through food.

Once you find the long-forgotten inner needs and work towards taking care of those inner needs, the need to find solace in food and binge eating will disappear because you would have found the real satisfaction of being your true self, which nothing else could fulfill.

Being Anchored To Your True Self

Being anchored to your true self simply means remaining aligned with your true self and the calling of the true self no matter how much the life situations around you should change. It means continually refocusing yourself to this single purpose of being that you truly are and leading a life that reflects your true self's calling. The journey is difficult only until you revive from your amnesia, only until you remember who you are and once you get connected with your true self, you will have access to an unlimited supply of inner strength. Regardless of how difficult life situations may turn out to be, nothing could really shake you because you would be having the contentment of being your true self. You will learn to transcend from the superficial life; a life in which you have been running around meaninglessly and traverse into a more meaningful life.

When you are anchored to your true self, your past traumas or bad memories will no more have that negative effect that it used to have on you anymore and it cannot push you to binge eating patterns anymore because you know that you have identified the needs of your true self and that you are busy focusing on those needs. Food cannot and will not distract you any more than it should for just existential reasons.

The Dynamics between Food, Body Image and Your True Self

Have you noticed how a baby learns to identify its mother first much before it learns to identify or recognize anyone else? It could be the mother or the primary caregiver that feeds the baby regularly helps the baby to recognize the source of food and at that stage food also means the basic sense of security for the baby. The baby may not be in a position to reason out about its own security and that just because it is with the mother or the primary caregiver it is safe. Rather, the baby just feels deep within this sense of security and that is why when someone else other than the mother or the primary caregiver carries the baby they scream their lungs out.

In other words, food is synonymous to love and security for the baby. The baby is not attached to the food but to the person that provides the food. If this initial relationship and attachment should be affected in some way due to whatever reasons the baby will start feeling insecure and it will soon start developing an attachment with food instead of developing an attachment to the person that provides food as it did in the previous instances.

Food was the very first expression of love and security for the baby. When the person associated with food disappears or is no more cordial, loving and caring then the baby starts missing the love that it used to enjoy and the sense of security that it used to experience in the presence of the person associated with food. As the baby grows up, it learns to find the love and security that it is missing in the food itself. So whenever this person wants to experience love and wants to feel safe and secure, use food as their solace and a source of comfort.

There is a deeper need that you are trying to address and attend to; what is that deeper need that you are trying to address when you reach out to food? Will food be able to gratify the deep-seated needs of your true self? These are some of the most crucial questions that you need to constantly ask yourself and you need to find answers.

When you learn the deep-seated needs of your true self, you will instantly realize that food is not your road to satisfaction and that is why you do not feel satisfied even when you gobble abnormal amounts of food.

If you have forgotten your true self and who you really are, waste no time in rediscovering your true self. It is high time that you responded to the needs of your true self, which have been long forgotten. Here are a few things that you could do to get in touch with your real self.

Allow yourself some quiet time and go through the following process and at the end of which you are likely to have a better connection with your true self.

Ask yourself the following question:

Who am I?

If the answer that you come up with is your name, then you should know that your name is not you. The name is just a label. Even without that label you can 'be' in the existential sense of the word 'be'.

If your name is not you, then who are you? What makes you 'YOU'? What signifies you? What are the qualities that make you as a person? What is your purpose on this earth? What is the higher purpose of your own existence? When you understand your own higher purpose, you will get to see things in a better light. Your life will never be the same again. All along you thought you have been running frantically towards achieving your so-called 'goals'. When you juxtapose your goals with your higher purpose, you will be able to see whether you are after the right things or whether you are running in the wrong direction.

What should you be doing to meet your higher purpose in life?

Is your current lifestyle and whatever you are doing taking you closer to achieving your higher purpose? What should you be doing to reach that higher purpose? What changes are required in your life? Are you ready to make those changes?

When you have made those changes how different would your life be? What would have changed?

Put yourself through this little exercise and ask yourself these self-revealing questions and be honest with your responses. This will help you get connected with your true self and your true self's deeper needs and urges. As long as you are going to turn a blind eye towards these goals you are going to feel empty and feel that everything that you are doing is meaningless after a certain point of time. Once you align yourself with your true self and start living a life that moves towards achieving the needs of your true self, you will experience that sense of satisfaction and contentment, which have been missing in your life all along.

Nurture Your True Self

Now that you have rediscovered your 'True Self' and identified or at least learning to identify the needs of that true self, it is of paramount importance to nurture your true self, which you have been ignoring all along.

For most of us our work life would be taking the toll out of us, leaving very little time for ourselves. Not everyone is lucky enough to have a career that aligns with the needs of our true self. We take up jobs that we do not necessarily love or like but nonetheless, we continue holding on to that job as we have our financial commitments. All along that is what you have been doing; if you have the luxury of changing your career and making a career out of your passions, then explore the possibilities of the same immediately. It would be one of the best ways of nurturing your true self. Every day you would wake up with unlimited energy to do things that you love doing.

If changing your career is not an option at least dedicate some time every day for your own passions and for things that your true self loves to do. Invest time in yourself and that is the best investment that you could possibly make. Never complain that you have no time for things that you like to do. Life would be meaningless if you do not have time for things that you love doing. What is the point in leading such a life? Make a timetable, find time for yourself and spend at least 60 minutes every day for things that you are passionate about and see how life changes. You will be able to heal yourself fully from your emotional eating issues and the scars that it has caused by nurturing your true self.

Chapter 10
Your Road to Recovery

You have learned a great deal about yourself and the reasons why you were behaving the way you were. You have also been connected with your true self and with the needs of your true self. These are your first steps in the road to recovery. This should give you a great sense of hope that at last there is light at the end of the tunnel and that you are not doomed.

Now that you have reconnected with your true self, a complete realignment is required to sustain your efforts. You are liberated psychologically with all the soul search that you have done and with the findings of your soul search. Your biology, however, will need time to rewire itself to embrace a life that is constituted of healthy eating response and a better way of dealing with your emotions.

Remember binge eating or emotional eating does not make you a bad person or make you inferior in any way. Just because you were responding to your inner needs in a specific way, it does not mean your self-worth is reduced. You are still precious, and this universe needs your contribution. Therefore, you had better be ready to make a difference!

Food Brings Joy

Remember food certainly brings joy! Eating good food is a pleasurable experience! Our brain is wired to feel good when you eat good food. All these have been designed millions of years ago and these impulses and responses have their own existential purposes. It is because of these impulses that we, the human race, is still on this planet. So food is not bad, but how we deal with it is what makes the results obtained good or bad.

As long as we are eating healthy food and as long as we know the limits and keep to the limits, the results will be good because it would be meeting the existential purpose that we were talking about a moment ago. On the other hand, when we go off-limits even the healthiest food that we consume could have a negative impact because it is not meeting the existential purposes rather it is going against the existential purpose and the results would be bad.

Therefore, just because you were going off-limits and producing results that were not so good it does not make food a 'bad' element or the fact that food can bring joy into your life. The goal here is to learn how to eat right and reclaim that joy of eating well. All along food has been an adversary in your life but you can change all that lot more easily as you have reframed your thinking and understood clearly what your real needs are. So there is no need to treat food as your enemy any longer.

There is a reason why our brain triggers the reward pathway when we eat food and makes it a pleasurable experience. In other words, it is in design that we should enjoy the eating experience. So it is not always about the nutrition and the numbers, there is more to food and you must enjoy complete fulfillment when you eat along with the nourishment that you get for your body.

You Are a Joyful Eater

Yes, this is what you need to believe in and tell yourself from now on; you are a joyful eater. There is no need to feel guilty when you experience that joy when you eat. Each one of us has a different physical constitution and lifestyle. You need to select the food that you eat and how much you eat based on your physical constitution and the demands of your body so that you stay healthy and active. You are the best judge to determine what is best for your body based on your specific bodily requirements. Have the liberty to choose your food and the quantity but do it responsibly.

Becoming and being a joyful eater is going to take some time, especially with what you have gone through. Remember we were staying healthy as a human race for millions of years when now dietician was around; diets and diet plans are meant to bring a balance in the food that we eat, but they are by no means absolute standards. It is important that you are not made to feel guilty by these diet plans. Listen to your body, the messages it continually sends you and be a mindful eater instead of feeling guilty that you are deviating from some diet plan. Let your focus on the diet plans change the way you experience food.

For once, stay away from calorie counting and your preoccupation with the list of good food and bad food. The mantra of a joyful eater is, 'Eat what is right for the body and enjoy what you eat.' This mantra contains everything, what you eat, how much you eat and how frequently you eat. When you follow this mantra, you cannot go wrong. While you are following this mantra – be totally present when you are eating so that you know what you are eating and what flavors are at play in your mouth. Cherish the flavors!

All along, you have failed to listen to your body, and it is high time that relearn how to listen to your body. Listening to your body is going to be an important skill that you are going to need as a joyful eater.

While you are trying to unlearn your past behaviors and relearn new skills, you are going to be challenged by the anecdotal food confusions with respect to what to eat and what not to eat. You would have gained this knowledge about good food and bad food from various sources right from your childhood from your parents, friends, your weight loss coaches, food experts, from books, from the internet and so on. The problem here is that all these advices and recommendations are not taking into consideration what is specifically good for your body. These are general recommendations. Do not allow these general recommendations lead to food confusions. Most of what you eat thinking as a good diet is nothing but fad diets. These diet programs result in disordered eating because you will come across diametrically opposite recommendations. You have low-fat diets that tell you to stay away from all fat-rich food and alongside you will also have this high fat keto diet that asks you to gobble chunks of butter. If you keep following these diet programs, you will certainly get confused and totally lose your ability to decide on your own what is good for your body and your ability to listen to your body.

Most of your food habits were picked up when you were young. Depending on what kind of parent or caregiver you grew up with, your later food habits and your approach to food would be determined. If you had a parent or caregiver who is very finicky about food and diet, you are likely to take after them as an adult. On the other hand, if you came from a family that had a healthy approach and outlook towards food then you are likely to take a similar approach as an adult. Remember, as an adult you have the freedom to decide what to keep and what to throw away. Not everything you picked up when you were young is good and useful. You should be able to use your discretion and revisit your own eating habit, keeping in mind what is good for your body.

As a joyful eater, opt for a wholesome and well-balanced diet and do not be worried about counting calories or about diet plans.

The Joy of Movement

Most of us lead a sedentary lifestyle and for most of us the longest walks are from the doorway to their car. We spend the entire day right at our desk and we call it work. Yes, for sure our lifestyle has changed a great deal from those days as hunters and gatherers. Those days we did not have to work in today's sense of the word 'work'. Nevertheless we were not sedentary because we had to be agile between meals, we kept moving from one food source to the next. Whatever food we consumed gave us, the energy that we needed to continue with the search. In other words, our body used all the energy produced by the food that we consumed. So a fine balance was maintained.

With all the automation and with all the mechanization today, we are proud that we do not have to do anything even as much as lifting our little finger. We can have our food delivered at our doorsteps and our food served at our tables. We get things done sitting right at our desk and at the click of a button. It is all good but in all these, what we have lost is the 'movement'. As a joyful eater, we might consume what is right for the body and what we enjoy but with your current lifestyle, your body is not given a chance to use the energy that it produces from the food you enjoy. The body does not know how to deal with this excess energy that it produces and what to do with the surplus. It accumulates everything as stored fat because it is wired to anticipate the worst, what if there is no food the next meal or for a few days?

You need to focus on giving your body what it has lost through your current lifestyle. Yes, you need to give back your body the 'movement' that it needs to keep you fit and healthy. As soon as we make a mention of movement, you do not have to start looking for expensive workout equipment online depleting your bank balance. Try to enjoy the natural movement of your body. Redesign your life so that there is natural movement instead of having to artificially introduce movement in the name of workout or exercise. There is a general aversion to exercise among many people. For many people, it has a negative ring to it.

You should consider yourself lucky if you enjoyed your workouts and you enjoyed exercising. Not many people love this experience but if they are adhering to their workout plan, it is out of sheer force because if they do not things could get worse. This is no good disposition to exercise. If you are going to have this negative disposition, then every day your mind is going to race through all possible excuses that it could give to stay away from the gym and from exercising. If you hate it so much then you should not be doing it. You might wonder, "If I am not going to work out or exercise how I am going to be healthy?" This is one of those misconceptions that most of us grow up with like broccoli is good for your health.

No Need to Exercise

When I say there is no need to exercise, I certainly do not mean natural movement but what the entire weight loss industry is trying to push on you in the form of weight loss equipment and workout plans. If exercising is a painful experience or if it is making you feel unhappy, then you do not have to do it.

However, as a joyful eater, if you want to be healthy, you need to ensure that there is enough movement in your life. Without adequate movement you are not going to reach those optimal levels of physical fitness and well-being. There are myriad ways to bring in natural movement back into your life.

- Walk to your local store or cycle to your local store instead of driving if it is within ten minutes reach by walk or cycling

- Take the stairs if you just need to climb two floors. If you need to reach the 32nd floor, take the stairs for the first two floors and get on to the escalator on the second floor.

- Mow your own lawn instead of calling lawn moving service

- Maintain a small garden at your backyard and grow your own food

- Play with your kids

- Become a member of the local tennis club and enjoy a game or two every week.

- Go for a swim

- Take your dog for a walk

You could come up with countless such activities that could bring natural movement into your life that do not make the whole activity or experience painful. You know your lifestyle better, do some paper and pen work and list all the possible ways through which you could bring natural movement into your sedentary lifestyle. You just need to sit for a moment to identify these opportunities in your current lifestyle without having to worry about lack of time. Of course, if required you could certainly make time for these things and everything boils down to priorities. All of us have time to attend to our top priorities in life and you too sure do!

What Is Stopping You from Bringing Natural Movement in To Your Life

At times, we would sincerely desire for a change. In this case, you might sincerely desire to bring change by bringing as much natural movement into your life as possible. However, for some unknown reason, you never get to make those changes that are required to bring natural movement into your life. If that is what you are experiencing then there could be possible deep-seated emotional blocks that are preventing you from embracing a lifestyle with abundant scope for natural movements.

If you have any such emotional blocks, you need to identify them and address them. Asking a series of crucial questions and answering them will help you get connected with yourself and overcome those emotional blocks.

When you are answering these questions do not think too much, just get hold of the first thought that comes instead of rationalizing things too much. Most importantly, you should be completely true to yourself and be honest with your responses.

- What feelings do the very thought of natural movement / exercise bring to you?

- What is causing or triggering those feelings? Can you go back in time when you experienced these feelings while exercising or working out?

- Can you recollect any past negative experiences that you think is making you feel this way about movement and exercise?

- What are the assumptions that you were holding in your head for you to feel this way?

- Can you now see that those assumptions are not valid assumptions and that there is no need for you to feel that way because most of it revolved around your assumptions?

By allowing yourself to work through the above series of questions and answering them honestly, this will help you gain more clarity, which in turn is likely to remove all possible aversions that you are likely to have against exercising and movement in general. Removing all such emotional blocks is an essential part of your journey towards recovery.

Dealing with Stress

We have already seen in the earlier chapters at great lengths, how stress leads to eating disorders. Your recovery journey cannot possibly be complete before you have acquired adequate skills to manage your stress, which is one of the major stimulators or triggers that got the binge eating patterns started. You might have managed to identify the needs of your true self and to come to the realization that food is not the real answer to your deep-seated needs, but it does not automatically give you the skills required to handle your stress in a healthy way. As long as you do not learn to deal with stress, which has been the most powerful switch in causing binge-eating responses, you are not fully out of the danger zone.

No one can today aspire to lead a life that is totally free from stress. Today's lifestyle has made stress part and parcel of life. At its best we could only learn to manage it better but not totally avoid it. So in this context, it is vital that you have a complete understanding of what is stress in your case because stress means so many different things to people. What is stressful for one may be something enjoyable for another person. Each one of us has our own set of parameters to classify the daily happenings as stress or as fun. One of the important questions that you need to ask therefore is, "What is stress?" You need to make sure that you are answering this question in a very subjective way based on your life situation and what causes you stress. The goal here is to ensure that you do not try to manage your stress through food. There are other better ways to manage your stress and you just need to be creative. Let us explore various ways to manage stress in a healthy way.

What is the definition of stress? This is an emotional state whereby one is feeling pressurized and tensed by their life circumstances. The life circumstances that make one feel stressed varies from person to person. For some, going on a trip would be an enjoyable experience and they look forward to the trip; whereas for someone else, it would be a highly stressful thing because they are worried about all the preparations that they need to make, the unfamiliar places that they have to visit and so on. It is important that you do not generalize things here because the person who is stressed about going on a trip could feel this way only when they go on a business trip. The same person would be very relaxed and excited when they are traveling with their family. In this case 'the trip' is not the stress but there is something other than the trip that is associated with the trip is what is making one stressed.

When you are learning to manage your stress, it is important that you understand clearly what is making you feel stressed. The above person who is stressed going on business trips would rule out the fact that they have the ability to get excited about going on a trip as long as it is not a business trip. This is because they simply jump to conclusions and fail to pay attention to details. When you fail to pay attention to details, you are likely to direct your energy in the wrong direction and as a result may not manage your stress effectively.

If you want to manage your stress effectively, then you should first gain a complete understanding regarding what causes stress in your case. It is best to list all those factors that you think leads you to feel stressed. It could be your financial status, monthly bills, kids, back to school season, approaching deadline at work and so on. List everything that normally stresses you out. After listing go over the list again asking whether you could make an absolute statement about these areas that make you feel stressed. For example, in the above example, in case of this person who gets stressed about business trips and not with family trips, he or she cannot make an absolute statement about going on trips and say, "Going on a trip always stresses me out!" for the sheer reason it is not always. There are exceptions in this person's own life whereby they are not experiencing any stress at all when they go on a family trip. You need to drill down further to what exactly is making you feel stressed. Only when you have that kind of clarity you will be able to address the real issues or else you will be continually be missing your target.

If you are not even clear what causes you stress then how do you hope to manage it? Your efforts would be nothing but taking shots in the dark. When you do not have effective stress management skills, then you are going to remain in a stressful state for prolonged periods. This, in turn, would induce secretion of cortisol, which triggers a stress-eating response. It is important therefore you invest enough time to analyze your own life carefully and list the real stressors so that you could manage it effectively.

Ways to Manage Stress

One of the mistakes most people make when it comes to dealing with their stress is to dwell more and more on the issue that is making them stressed trying to overcome the situation. Instead of aggravating the situation by dwelling more on the issues, try to take a break from the situation with positive distractions. When you are in the middle of the issues your mind loses its ability to think creatively and its ability to be resourceful. When you take a break, get involved with some other activity that is making you feel positive or at least normal, you will gain back your original acumen on problem-solving and troubleshooting.

All of us must have a set of de-stressors that we could use when we are stressed. It could be just about anything and the only criteria are that it should be a healthy approach and that it should be safe.

It could be something as simple as,

- Listening to music
- Playing a music instrument
- Taking a way
- Going on long drive
- Meeting a friend
- Playing your favorite sport
- Gardening
- Reading and the list simply extends...

When you have such a positive distraction, the need for your body to find its comfort in food will automatically disappear. Only when you have not planned in advance what you would do or how you would go about dealing with stress, you will slide into binge eating. Stress eating is a self-defeating approach and it does not make you feel better on the long run even though it gives you a temporary sense of relief.

Manage your stress well and you will automatically be managing your eating issues better.

Chapter 11
Inner Nurturing Forever

You have come a long way! It was not easy for you to come this far! Having come this far, you would certainly not want all your efforts that you have put in to become futile. You certainly want all these to stay with you and to bear fruit all your life.

Overcoming your binge eating or emotional eating or stress eating is not at all easy. You have seen that it has so many pieces, which you carefully managed to put together until you figured out fully what is going on and managed to see the bigger picture. If you think reaching up to this point was challenging, yes, it would have been but what is going to be an even bigger challenge is to remain there.

What you need to understand and accept is that, setbacks and failures and bad days are part of this journey. When they do pop up, you should be ready to face them as if you knew that they are coming, but you are equipped enough now to face them with courage. Yes, that is the whole difference now; you are better equipped with the knowledge about your true self and about your inner needs. Even if there are setbacks and even if it looks that you are trailing back to your old ways things are a lot better now because you know you the way back.

Remain connected with your inner nurturer, your best friend and guide. You are going to need the support of this inner nurturer more than ever. You may not be able to fall back on your family or friends when things do not go the way you expected and when you find yourself at the verge of your weakness, but you can rely on your inner nurturer for support.

Listen to the voice of the inner nurturer telling you that you are amazing! Let the inner nurturer reassure you saying, "I am here, and you are going to be OK." When you fail here your inner nurturer telling you, "I can understand but you put up a good fight! You will do better the next time!"

You need to approach things more realistically and set practical goals for yourself. One of the reasons why many people who try to stop binge-eating run into issues is that they feel heartbroken once they fail. They cannot take failures and setbacks. They are very harsh on themselves. Instead, of hearing the voice of the inner nurturer they hear the voice of the inner critic, "How can you be so stupid to throw away all the work you have done so far and give into the moment of weakness?" Not letting the inner critic condemn you is very important. If you expect things to change overnight, then your inner critic will gain an upper hand. Instead if you allow your psyche and your biology to handle things in their own way at their reasonable pace, you will not be heartbroken when things go wrong with your efforts. You are likely to fail, and you will, but it certainly does not mean you are a failure. It just means that you need to pick it up and start all over.

It is important to take a loving and compassionate approach. You need to be compassionate with yourself but not self-pity. If the inner critic gains upper hand then you are likely to feel sorry for yourself and end up in self-pity, which is not going to put you in a resourceful state. Instead, if you let the inner-nurturer support you, you are likely to be in a more resourceful state.

Make Your Inner Nurturer Strong

Most of us grow up with hearing the voice of the critic and so it is so easy for us to hear the negative words of the critic. On the other hand, we are not used to the inner nurturer, that is why you are not familiar with this voice, and therefore it becomes little challenging to get connected with this voice. Even when we manage to get connected with this voice, it is weak and not all that strong. When it is not all that strong, it will also not be all that convincing. When it says, "It is OK to fail!" you tend to rebel saying "It is not OK to fail!"

It needs some getting used to your inner nurturer and its supportive and consoling voice. The more sensitive you become to your inner nurturer's voice, the stronger it will get. It does not matter that during the initial stages even if it not all that convincing as it may sound, just allow yourself to believe in the inner nurturer. After all you need to rely on someone, a friend or a family member or someone that you could confide in and that someone could very well be your inner nurturer. Strengthening the voice of the inner nurturer will be to your great advantage because it is only through continued inner nurturing it is possible for you hold on to healthy eating patterns. Especially when you know that the journey to recovery is not a sprint but a marathon.

How Can You Make Things Easy For Yourself?

It is important to find various ways and means to make things easy for yourself. There are a few important things that you should start doing immediately. It is not enough planning these things, but all these will be of use to you only when you implement them right away.

One day at a time - It is relatively easier to cope with the challenges that you are likely to face in your journey if you just plan for today. Instead of making a long-term plan and telling yourself, 'I will ensure that I will not give into binge eating for the next five years,' keep the target closer to you so that you will not be burdened with the thought of having to take control of yourself for the next five years. Living one day at a time successfully will of course easily get past the next five years. So plan for today and stick to your plan. Make a new plan the next day as if it is your first day. Do not unnecessarily burden your inner self.

Do something for your true self every day Your true self is often left orphaned when you are busy with your rat race. You tend to attend to so many other things but fail to attend to the needs of your true self and worse still you totally forget about your true self and who you are. Every day, ask yourself what you are going to do for your true self, the real you. Yes, of course, you will be busy at work, you will have tight deadlines and you will have so many other excuses. All those things are only taking care of just one aspect of your life – that is making money or meeting your sustenance needs. Do not make this aspect your whole life. Give time for the other aspects of your life.

Get connected with your long-forgotten dreams – When you were growing up you had so many dreams and aspirations that were originally aligned with your true self. It is never too late, no matter how old you are now, you can make at least a part of that dream come true. Get started today, do not delay any further. These are your real needs and how can your life meaningful when you do not even have time for your real needs? Get started right away, do something today that will help you get one step closer to the dreams and desires of your true self. Take one step closer to your dream each day and this will make you feel good, feel content and feel gratified. When you do this, you would not be looking for comfort in food, alcohol, sex or addictive substances.

Train yourself to enjoy and appreciate the little things in life

Your life is full of little things; why even the entire universe moves at the pace of one moment at a time. How could anyone make life meaningful and make it big if they are going to let these moments slip through their fingers? The joy of life is in appreciating and enjoying these little moments.

Make mindfulness your way of living – If you can do this, then all your life's problems will disappear with time. Most of us feel the way that we do just because we engage in so many activities mindlessly and this results in a series of issues. One thing leads to the other, even before we could realize what is happening, we get sucked into it and we lose ourselves in the commotion that we have created for ourselves. We could do away with all these agonies by practicing mindfulness. When it comes to mindfulness, we try to compartmentalize it to just few minutes of our life. The best way to practice mindfulness is rather to let it slip through all aspects of life. No matter what we do, no matter how trivial the task that we are at, if only we could handle them all with mindfulness, we will be able to lead a more fulfilling life and we are also likely to have a better control over our own eating responses.

The Recovery Phase

You are in a recovery phase right now and during this phase you are likely to experience a series of changes. You need to be physically and mentally prepared for these changes. You are going to surprise yourself daily.

As you continue your journey to recovery, be prepared to face these patterns:

There will be moments or days when you feel extremely confident that you would be able to pull through that day without succumbing to your older weaknesses pertaining to eating and you will manage to pull through as you expected.

There will be days that you do not feel alright about and you would not be sure whether you would be able to make it that day. Just as you had guessed you would have given into eating binge that day.

There will be days that you would be confident that you are in control but to your disappointment you would have failed miserably that day.

There will be days in which you would be almost certain that you would fail, but to your surprise you would have managed to get through that day without giving into your weakness.

Instead of trying to analyze the reasons and why such things happen, just move on. Going over the day analyzing and scrutinizing it with a microscope will only make you feel bad and for no reason. You know that you are clear with your goal and with where you want to go. Keep to your journey practicing mindfulness, paying attention to your body sensations, remaining connected with your real self and meeting the needs of the inner self. As far as this journey is concerned, do not stop to scrutinize every minor setback because it is not useful.

You just need to be mentally prepared and accept the fact that every day is going to be different and every day is going to present a new challenge. If you could anticipate that challenge well and good but if it comes as a surprise despite all your efforts, don't sweat on it too much deal with it and get past that challenge. You have many other better things to focus upon in your life.

Plan Your Weekly Menu

You might as well want to consider planning your weekly menu and make it a habit so that you are not leaving things to chances. When you know what you are going to eat for each meal, you can do better with weekly shopping. Instead of loading your shopping cart with loads of things that you do not intend to use, you could come back with smaller shopping bags every week. This will also avoid unnecessary food wastage and at the same time save you from unnecessary temptation.

There is yet another advantage in planning your weekly menu. You will be able to balance your diet even when you ate things that you love. Make sure that you get enough proteins, carbs and fat that your body needs. If you do not plan your weekly menu, you are going to pick things in a random fashion and the chances are that you do not get to eat a well-balanced diet. Remember, the goal here is not to put you on to any specific diet or to curtail yourself from certain types of food. It is just about planning what you would prefer to eat for each meal and how to bring a certain kind of balance. Whether or not you are dieting your body is going to need the nutrition that it needs, and you have no option but to give your body what it needs. You are just embracing a systematic approach. Do not read too much into your weekly meal planning. To make this meal planning even more enticing, you could first the list of things that you love eating and listing them under different food categories such as protein, carbs, fat, etc. Once you have them all, see what is missing and which section of your menu is weak and include items that will strengthen the weak segment but still with items that you like to eat. If only you could make this approach your habit, it will bring amazing benefits.

Moreover, people who plan their meal this way say that it gives them great peace of mind because they do not have to worry each meal wondering what they are to eat. These pre-planned meals will certainly simplify your life because you are do not have to go through the long list of items before you prepared your meal each day and cross check whether you have everything required to prepare the dish. When you plan your meals you are also simultaneously planning your weekly shopping.

Notice the Good Things

What is even more important is to keep track of your own progress. Notice the good things as you move on. You notice that you are now taking smaller portions of food. You would no longer be sneaking food. You will know that you are full now, you need to stop, and you will stop. All these are signs that you are moving in the right direction. As the days go by, you will notice that all these things are taking place without having to put in any special efforts. After some time you will realize that you are not even stopping to notice how much food you are serving yourself, but you have been keeping to decent portions. Yes, you would gradually move to this effortless state of victory.

Along with all these, you will also notice that all your XL / L sized outfits are becoming loose and that you have start pulling out your M sized dresses? Have you not been craving for these changes for a long time? Do not fail to notice that these good changes are happening in your life. It is important that you take notice of them and consciously register these changes because it is important for your brain to get this concrete feedback. You are taking on a new self and this is the most beautiful phase of your journey, a phase when all your efforts translate into results.

You will notice all such changes not only with your response to food and with the dresses you wear but also with the way that people look at you and treat you. They cannot help but notice the change that is happening in you and with you. Some will generously compliment you and others will notice but not be generous enough to give you a compliment. Be prepared for all kinds of reactions. Do not set any expectations on how others should respond to the changes that are happening in you and let it not bother you too much. If they give a compliment, you take it gracefully and if they don't, do not be disappointed.

Of course, you are going to start feeling lighter and have more energy throughout the day. Enjoy these changes and you know that you deserve this feeling! When you are losing weight once you start having a better control over your eating pattern and your response to food, you will notice that your skin is saggy. This is very normal and there are a number of ways to deal with this physiological change. You might want to increase your natural movements so that the entire body gets enough exercise to tighten up the skin. There are also firming creams in the market that you could try. There are several ways to tighten your saggy skin.

The amount of money you spend on food will also come down dramatically. You would be happy to see smaller credit card bills. You are likely to have more money to spare for other things. You could use the extra cash to give yourself a treat in a spa or to go for a massage. If you are planning to give yourself a treat, choose things that do not involve food and drink. You could also use the extra cash to meet the needs of your true self.

Often people who are on their road to recovery do not plan for all these good things. They only focus on the negative things and plan to deal with them. For a change, you now start planning for these good things as well and decide how you are going to handle these changes. The days are not far off for you to experience everything that we listed above in the last section on noticing the good things. Don't you think it is nice to focus on those good things that have already started coming your way and as you are getting one step closer to these nicer things? Yes, of course, it is wonderful to have your eye on the treasure!

Conclusion

Whatever has happened in your life has happened for a reason. In this journey, you have managed to get connected with your true self. Getting over your binge eating issues is just a tiny episode of your life; do not make it into your entire life's story. Everyone that is walking past you has one or other such episode or episodes in their lives too. The good news is that you have had the courage to face it and address it. Now you are in control of your life and that is what matters now.

It is not enough to get connected with your true self and to understand the needs of your true self. Your true self has a special calling and a special vocation. There is a higher purpose for your existence. You need to approach your life with that higher purpose in mind starting today! You might have already found that higher purpose or you could still be exploring. Allow yourself to be steered by that higher purpose and you will notice your life take on a new meaning and taking you to amazing places.

There are millions of people who have lost themselves in the frantic 'running around' who need help and support. You could be that support that they are not even looking for because they do not even realize that they are in need of help.

Make your journey count for something!

www.ingramcontent.com/pod-product-compliance
Lightning Source LLC
Chambersburg PA
CBHW070940080526
44589CB00013B/1580